THE GIRL WHO WAS ON FIRE

THE

GIRL WHO
WAS ON FIRE

Edited by
LEAH WILSON

Your Favorite Authors on
Suzanne Collins'
Hunger Games Trilogy

An Imprint Of Benbella Books, Inc. • Dallas, Texas

Smart Pop is an Imprint of BenBella Books, Inc.
10300 N. Central Expressway, Suite 400
Dallas, TX 75231
www.benbellabooks.com
www.smartpopbooks.com
Send feedback to feedback@benbellabooks.com

Printed in the United States of America
10 9 8 7 6 5 4 3

Library of Congress Cataloging-in-Publication Data is available for this title.
ISBN 978-1- 935618-04-1

Copyediting by Erica Lovett and Heather Butterfield
Proofreading by Scott Cain
Cover design by Faceout Studio
Text design and composition by Neuwirth & Associates, Inc.
Printed by Bang

Distributed by Perseus Distribution
http://www.perseusdistribution.com/

To place orders through Perseus Distribution:
Tel: (800) 343-4499
Fax: (800) 351-5073
E-mail: orderentry@perseusbooks.com

CONTENTS

INTRODUCTION

You could call the Hunger Games a series that is—like its heroine—on fire. But its popularity, in itself, is nothing new. We live in an era of blockbuster young adult book series: Harry Potter, Twilight, now the Hunger Games. It's more unusual these days for there *not* to be a YA series sweeping the nation.

All of these series have certain things in common: compelling characters; complex worlds you want to spend time exploring; a focus on family and community. But the Hunger Games is, by far, the darkest of the three. In Twilight, love conquers all; Bella ends the series bound eternally to Edward and mother to Renesmee, without having to give up her human family or Jacob in the process. In Harry Potter, though there is loss, the world is returned to familiar stability after Voldemort's defeat, and before we leave them, we see all of the main characters happily married, raising the next generation of witches and wizards. In the Hunger Games, while Katniss may conclude the series similarly married and a mother, the ending is much more bittersweet. Her sister and Gale are both lost to her in different but equally insurmountable ways. The world is better than it was, but there are hints that this improvement is only temporary—that the kind of inhumanity we saw in the districts under Capitol rule is the true status quo, and that the current peace is ephemeral, precious, something toward which Panem will always have to struggle.

In other words, the Hunger Games ends in a way that feels surprisingly *adult*—bleak, realistic, as far from wish fulfillment as one can imagine. Such a conclusion only emphasizes something YA readers have known for years: that there is serious, engaging, transformative work going on in YA literature. The Hunger Games is more than Gale versus Peeta; there's so much more at stake in this series than love (and so much more at stake *in loving*, here, as well). The series takes on themes of power and propaganda, trauma and recovery, war and compassion. It's about not just learning one's power, but learning the limits of one's power as well.

Because at its core, the Hunger Games is a coming-of-age story, and not just for Katniss—it's a coming-of-age story for Panem, and in a way, for us, its readers, as well. The series pushes us to grow up and take responsibility both personally and politically for our choices: those Capitol residents we see milling through the streets in *Mockingjay*, the same Capitol residents who so raptly watched the Hunger Games on television year after year without recognizing the suffering that made it possible, are *us*. That's a heavy message to take away from any book series, but an important one for all of us—whether we ourselves would be shelved under Young Adult or not.

The pieces you're about to read don't cover everything in the Hunger Games series (they couldn't cover everything), but they do tease out at least a few of the series' most thought-provoking ideas. Together, they provide an extended meditation on the series and its world, on Katniss and our response to her, on love and family and sacrifice and survival. But you shouldn't take this to mean the anthology is always as serious as *Mockingjay* at it heaviest. There's humor, and warmth, and hope here, too. Each of our contributors has brought his or her own particular interests and expertise to exploring the series, and topics run the gamut from fashion to science to reality television and real-world media training.

Still, you'll find these essays tend to return to the same events and the same ideas over and over again. But each time we revisit them our perspective shifts—the same way reality in the series is constantly shifting—letting us interpret old events, old ideas, in new ways. As each writer passes the torch to the next, our contributors cover new ground while pushing our understanding of the Hunger Games as a whole further, toward a greater awareness of everything these books have to offer.

While editing this anthology, I was alternately surprised, fascinated, and moved to tears—a tribute not only to the Hunger Games series itself but also to the talented YA writers whose work is collected here. And I hope that you, too, will find something fresh to feel or think about in these pages—that *The Girl Who Was on Fire* encourages you to debate, question, and experience the Hunger Games in a whole new way.

Leah Wilson
December 2010

WHY SO HUNGRY FOR THE HUNGER GAMES?

Or, the Game of Making Readers Hungry for More, Why
Readers' Imaginations Caught Fire, and My Sad Inability
to Come Up with a Wordplay for *Mockingjay*

SARAH REES BRENNAN

The Hunger Games is, without question, a great series. Millions of
readers have stuck with Katniss Everdeen through three books, two
rounds of Games, and a war—and still can't get enough. If you're reading
this book, then none of this is news to you. But what is it about this
dystopian story that draws in readers of all ages and genres? Why have
these books enraptured a generation? It's no easy question to tackle,
but Sarah Rees Brennan suggests some very compelling answers.

As you can tell from all the atrocious puns in the title, this essay will be studying the elements in the Hunger Games trilogy that inspire its tremendous popularity. It's fascinating to analyze the mixture of elements that has caught readers' imaginations around the world. What is so alluring about the Hunger Games' particular mixture of adventure, romance, and philosophy? Many of the elements present in the series are familiar, so how does Suzanne Collins make it all seem fresh and compelling?

For a long time I avoided the Hunger Games because, well, I'd seen *Battle Royale*, thank you very much. (*Battle Royale* is a Japanese movie, based on the book of the same name by Koushun Takami, about high school students who are chosen by lottery to kill each other under new legislation introduced by a futuristic government.) I finally buckled under the weight of hearing everybody's enthusiastic recommendations for six months, and then I read the Hunger Games voraciously and was extremely annoyed when interrupted by such inconsequential things as "Christmas dinner." (God, Mom, did you not understand Katniss was being pursued by the mutts? You have several children, why does it always have to be about collecting the whole set all the time?)

So my assumption made an ass out of me, and I missed out on the Hunger Games for six months! My reason for avoiding the Hunger Games really was ridiculous, as we all know there are no brand-new plots under the sun: what really matters is the way you tell the stories and the passion you have for them. *Battle Royale*, as I've said, deals with children killing each other for the benefit of an audience and with the sanction of the government.

Ben Elton's adult comic novel *Dead Famous*, in which a murder happening on a reality TV show drives up the ratings and makes the show a phenomenon (and it turns out the producers planned it all along), deals with many of the same issues of human fascination with reality television, violence, and the question of how illusion can mingle with reality.

So there are no new ideas under the sun, and, if you ask Christopher Booker (author of *The Seven Basic Plots*), only seven plots in the world. What is it about Suzanne Collins' treatment of the idea that has struck such a chord with readers? A writer friend of mine, Justine Larbalestier (author of *Liar*), described the Hunger Games books as "sticky," meaning that they are compulsive reading. Once you have picked them up, it's difficult to stop reading: your attention does not wander, and your urge to find out what happens next does not falter.

Why is that? One reason is how deeply the Hunger Games goes into the questions of reality versus illusion and the examination of the media's current fascination with manufactured reality, as well as humanity's enduring fascination with violence. The idea of children killing each other is a horrible one to anyone, and yet so morbidly alluring. The evil presented by the Hunger Games is so terrible, and in this society so all-encompassing, that we watch Katniss' adventures with instantly evoked sympathy, horror, interest, and simple terror—because we cannot imagine how she is going to get out of this situation. Another thing that kept me reading compulsively was sheer interest in how the novel is structured: how does Suzanne Collins allay the very bleak premise of the Hunger Games enough so that we are not all carted, weeping softly, off to a lunatic asylum in the middle of *Catching Fire*, and how does she keep her characters sympathetic even when they are almost all, by necessity, murderers?

Anyone who speaks Latin (gets egged by the populace for being a nerd) must have wondered from the start if Panem was a reference to the Roman people's reported liking for bread and circuses—for instant gratification that would distract them from the harsher realities of life. This is confirmed in *Mockingjay*, but Collins has said in a recent interview that she had it in mind from the start, and thus must have had in mind the questions: Why is it that that, for thousands of years, we humans have been allured by and interested in violent death? And what do you do when the underpinning of your whole society is based on this fascination? The answer is destroy the society and build a new one, which is an overwhelmingly daunting task, especially for a child who has to fight endlessly just for her own survival.

The premise of the Hunger Games provides us not only with a set-up for nonstop action, in which not only are the heroine's life and the lives of the vast majority of the supporting characters in danger, but they and we possess a continuous awareness of both having and having to entertain an audience. Katniss is forced to go through with not one but two Hunger Games. In *The Hunger Games*, she is deeply aware of the audience because she knows playing on its sympathies by pretending love for Peeta will get the two the food and medicine they need to survive. In *Catching Fire*, the equation is even simpler—unless Katniss and Peeta give a convincing enough display of being madly in love, Snow will conclude that they are revolutionaries instead of lovers and have them executed. In each case, the weight of the populace's expectations weighs heavily on Katniss, influencing both her actions and her feelings. It is a deadly loop, as both Katniss and the audience discover. We the readers are aware that Katniss' audience is both enthralled by her pain and gullibly sucked in by her love story. Yet all the while we know that *we* are Katniss' real audience—and aren't we enthralled by her pain and sucked in by her love story? How gullible does that make us?

The message of the Hunger Games is that appearances are both deceiving and vitally important. It is Cinna, Katniss' stylist, who ties together Katniss and Peeta in the audience's eyes by making them hold hands: "Presenting ourselves not as adversaries but as friends has distinguished us as much as the fiery costumes" (*The Hunger Games*). Katniss first attracts attention with costumes cleverly designed by Cinna and his team, and the importance of appearance is underlined again when Cinna (who dies near the end of *Catching Fire*) administers a makeover *from beyond the grave* in *Mockingjay*. Here too is one thing that gives relief to the grim storyline of the Hunger Games. Katniss does not want to be dressed up, or enjoy dressing up; she has no interest in such things. But the readers who do can enjoy the lovingly described costumes and the idea of being made up to be someone more attractive, someone so compelling they could end up being the sole focus of an audience's attention, while the rest of the readers simply sympathize with Katniss during another trial.

In a way, the romantic subplot of the books reminds me of the makeover scenes. The romance intensifies the life-or-death tension of the books, because we know that Katniss and Peeta being able to appear to be in love is even more important than Katniss being able to appear beautiful—these illusions will save their lives. But it also provides relief: just like there are readers who would like to be transformed, there are readers who would like to be loved in the way Katniss is. Peeta loves her even though they have barely spoken, even though they hardly know each other. She has won his love from afar by doing nothing but being herself, fiercely struggling for her own survival and that of her family, and he loves her so much he is willing to lie, to kill, and to die for her. The reader never really doubts Peeta's love for Katniss, even when Katniss believes it is total illusion, and that not only provides a ray of light in the dark situation of the Hunger Games but endears both characters to us. Then we are shocked in *Mockingjay* when the one thing we did believe was real, Peeta's love, may be destroyed.

If many of us like the idea of being loved from afar without having to work for or even be aware of it, there is also Gale, Katniss' childhood friend and hunting companion. None of us want to be reduced to hunting desperately to feed our families, but if we were, it wouldn't hurt for one's trusty companion to be a good-looking, much-sought-after, and rather devoted member of the opposite sex. That leaves Katniss in a bit of a bind, of course—even if she does manage to survive, it seems that there is going to be a painful choice to make.

The romance also further displays the complexities of reality versus illusion: Suzanne Collins does not go the easy route of condemning illusion in favor of reality. Peeta, the golden boy of the series, the main character whose morality is the strongest and who is always the spokesperson for decency, is actually an accomplished liar, in the first book able to convince both the Career tributes and Katniss that he is a merciless killer. He is also able to use his skills as a baker to camouflage himself when wounded in the Games. As he puts it: "I guess all those hours decorating cakes paid off" (*The Hunger Games*).

Katniss, at first profoundly uncomfortable with deceit, by the end of *Mockingjay* ends up fooling the reader into thinking that she has agreed to the unthinkable—setting up a new Hunger Games—and thus become what she has been fighting against all this time. When she shoots Coin rather than Snow, we realize that this agreement was her means of getting the chance to execute Coin and end the idea for the new Hunger Games. We also realize that a very new Katniss Everdeen has evolved over the Hunger Games trilogy, one who has progressed from being able to fool nobody to one who can fool everybody, including us.

Gale may in fact be the most open and honest character in the books. "I never question Gale's motives while I do nothing but doubt [Peeta's]," says Katniss in *The Hunger Games*. Suzanne Collins pulls a neat trick with Gale: he advocates throughout the three books for retaliation against the injustice of their society. But we the reader, like Katniss, are not sure he entirely means what he says. Gale is on the sidelines and understandably frustrated while Katniss and Peeta spend all three books in the eye of the storm. "Back in the old days . . . Gale said things like this and worse. But then they were just words. Here, put into practice, they become deeds that can never be reversed" (*Mockingjay*). Suzanne Collins tells us how Gale is, and yet we do not quite realize it until the third book, when he turns his words into actions and thereby loses Katniss forever—by being the person he told her he was all along.

The major issue between Katniss and Gale in *Mockingjay* is precisely that Gale really does mean what he says. The reality of Gale—that he is so capable of hate and violence, that he is ultimately unable to protect Katniss' family—is the major problem between the two. Katniss' illusions about Gale—her thinking that he does *not* mean what he says—helps Gale's cause romantically. Likewise with the audience. Gale has very limited page time in the first two books, but he is a literary archetype. The tall, dark, and handsome, aloof and mysterious boy who really connects with you even though all the ladies want him is a very appealing type. The figure of the "baker," blond, sweet Peeta, is much less intrinsically alluring than the figure of the "hunter."

Gale's surface makes him extremely popular with readers, but the whole point of the Hunger Games is all the things going on beneath the surface.

It is an interesting juxtaposition, because if the problem between Katniss and Gale is reality, the problem between Katniss and Peeta is always illusion. Peeta is deceived by Katniss' feigned love in *The Hunger Games*, both are forced into play-acting in *Catching Fire*, and in *Mockingjay* Peeta's mental torture has had such an effect on him that he can no longer tell the difference between reality and illusion, between Katniss who he loves and his most deadly enemy. The other characters have to supply answers to Peeta's constant refrain of "Real or not real?" throughout *Mockingjay*. He cannot entirely trust their answers, and yet he has to because he cannot rely on his own perception. His position is horrifying, and yet it is just a magnified version of everyone's position in the Hunger Games—of our own positions as consumers of entertainment that pretends to reflect reality. The refrain "Real or not real?" is a simply a vocalization of the ultimate question of the Hunger Games, and it is a question without any definite answer.

War ends up having the same layers of deceit as the Hunger Games does. Early in *Mockingjay* the characters all come to the conclusion that Katniss is only convincing as a spokesperson when she herself is convinced by the situation: when it is real to her. So the rebellion has to set evocative scenes for Katniss, just as Snow and the Capitol do in the previous two books. Propaganda in war is even more important than in entertainment, and so the war we have known must happen from the start of the Hunger Games—a war to change this unbearable society—is portrayed as manufactured killing, as just another Hunger Games, and not much more real.

We never really do get a face for the antagonist: the closest we come is Snow, and not only does Katniss explicitly reject the chance to kill him, but his death is quite flippantly accomplished and dismissed by the narrative: "Opinions differ on whether he choked to death by laughing or was crushed by the crowd. No one really cares" (*Mockingjay*). There is no easy way to defeat the evil in the world of the Hunger Games. It is the evil inherent in all of us, and even at the end it is by no means certain that all the evil we have been shown will not spring up again. After all, as Plutarch tells Katniss, "We're fickle, stupid beings with poor memories and a great gift for self-destruction" (*Mockingjay*).

Katniss has a gift for destruction of both herself and others, which she realizes in *Mockingjay* makes her very like Gale. And yet she makes the decision not to be like Gale—not to kill Snow but to take out Coin, to eliminate the threat of violence in the future, rather than take revenge for violence in the past.

She also realizes that what she needs is someone who helps her be her better self, rather than someone who reflects her worst self: the guy less like her is actually the guy who's best for her. To a degree, Gale decides the issue for her: not that he doesn't love her, but that his actions in the war mean she will never be able to disassociate him from her sister's death. Fans of both boys can be happy, in that Gale is never actually rejected by Katniss. He recognizes her feelings, which have to do with Prim rather than Peeta, and bows out. Last we hear, he has a "fancy job" and Katniss speculates about his possible other romances. Gale seems to be doing just fine for himself, and indeed one has pictures of the rebellion reunions in which Gale shows up in a flashy sports car and says, "Katniss, baby, you could have got with all this." We, like Katniss, may feel a certain amount of regret at how things turned out, but we also see how feeding the fire of hate plays out with Gale, so we sympathize with Katniss both in her realization that she is similar to Gale and in how it informs her ultimate decision that Peeta is a better mate for her, which we see when their love is both verbally confirmed and physically consummated.

"Wait, what was that you just said?" I hear you cry. Don't worry, dear reader, I am not the lucky recipient of the Secret Naughty Edition of the Hunger Games. But Katniss wakes screaming in Peeta's arms, and then his lips are there to comfort her, and then "on the night I feel that thing again, the hunger that overtook me on the beach . . . So after . . . " (*Mockingjay*). After what, Katniss? Don't think we didn't notice the adroit dropping of the word "hunger" either. After the Games of Amore end, after the conclusion of the Hunger for Loooove, after their ardent quest to catch fire in the flames of passion, after—I'm sure nobody wants to hear me make a sexy joke involving *Mockingjay*'s title. Perhaps Katniss only refers to a truly excellent make-out session. Perhaps I am a filthy-minded creature from the gutter (perhaps there is no perhaps about that one). Anyway, they eventually have two kids, so I rest assured in the knowledge it's going to happen sometime.

Katniss and Peeta's romance has a very definite conclusion. In fact, overall the Hunger Games has a very final ending, in the manner of Harry Potter, which wound up the seven-book series nineteen years later, with the hero and several other characters established as married with children. Katniss and Peeta have aged at least fifteen years and have children, and their society has been successfully readjusted, the Hunger Games seemingly permanently eliminated, though their psyches remain scarred by war. The book is definitively closed, perhaps to remove any possibility of being tempted to write sequels that might spoil the arc of the books. Many of the most beloved series have very final endings and give their readers a resounding sense of closure, though this may be more cause than effect—because of their popularity, the author may feel he or she has to close the book on the series with no possibility of return. I feel C.S. Lewis still takes the cake with his ending for the Chronicles of Narnia, which is "the world ends, and everyone who isn't currently in that world dies in a train crash anyway—oh, except for that one chick"—but well played on a decisive finish, Ms. Collins!

The Hunger Games trilogy has an unsettling premise that combines action adventure with a social conscience, the wish-fulfillment of having two guys desperately in love with you, and a resoundingly conclusive ending. It also has a writer who selected her subject material carefully, and who by choosing a subject that fascinated her chose a subject that resonated with a great many other people. We sympathize with the characters, able to doubt them just enough to add to the suspense, as we fear Peeta is betraying Katniss in *The Hunger Games* and Katniss is supporting a new Hunger Games in *Mockingjay*, and yet we are able to trust them in extremis. Katniss never considers killing the young girl Rue in *The Hunger Games*; the worst lines are never crossed by our hero and heroine, which allows us to continue to care for them despite their violent actions. Suzanne Collins even provides us, through the romantic subplot, with an answer for the overlap between reality and illusion. Katniss' many deceptions do eventually accomplish good: the Hunger Games are over, and despite all Katniss' losses society is at least improved. When Peeta asks Katniss at the end of *Mockingjay*, "You love me, real or not real?" and she answers, "Real," we know this was not always true. Illusion can become reality. Love is real now.

Even though the audience knows Katniss, Peeta, and the Hunger Games are all not real, we still believe that answer is true.

SARAH REES BRENNAN *was born in Ireland by the sea, where she spent her schooldays secretly reading books rather than learning Irish. That paid off, as she is now the author of the Demon's Lexicon trilogy, a series about attractive troubled brothers and all the fierce ladies and evil magicians they know, the first book of which received three starred reviews and was a Top Ten ALA book. Her next book, cowritten with Justine Larbalestier, comes out in 2012.*

TEAM KATNISS

▶

JENNIFER LYNN BARNES

Who doesn't love a good love triangle—especially one involving guys like Peeta and Gale? Finding out which boy Katniss would end up with was an important moment—and for some readers the most important moment—in the series. But, as Jennifer Lynn Barnes reminds us, amid all the talk of who Katniss would *choose*, we sometimes forgot to think about who Katniss actually *is*. Barnes looks at Katniss independent of potential love interests and provides a convincing alternative to Team Peeta and Team Gale: Team Katniss.

These days, it seems like you can't throw a fish in a bookstore without hitting a high-stakes love triangle—not that I recommend the throwing of fish in bookstores, mind you (it annoys the booksellers—not to mention the fish), but it certainly seems like more and more YA heroines are being faced with a problem of abundance when it comes to the opposite sex. While I am a total sucker for romance (not to mention quite fond of a variety of fictional boys myself), I still can't help but wonder if, as readers, we're becoming so used to romantic conflict taking center stage that we focus in on that aspect of fiction even when there are much larger issues at play.

No book has ever made me ponder this question as much as Suzanne Collins' Hunger Games trilogy—in part because it seems like everyone I know has very strong feelings about which boy is the best fit for Katniss, but also because the books themselves contain a commentary on the way audiences latch onto romance, even (and maybe especially) when lives are at stake. To survive her first Hunger Games, Katniss has to give the privileged viewers in the Capitol exactly what they want—a high-stakes romance featuring star-crossed lovers and unthinkable choices. Given that readers of the Hunger Games trilogy are granted insider access to Katniss' mind, life, and obligations, it seems somewhat ironic that in the days leading up to the release of *Mockingjay*, the series was often viewed the same way—with readers on "Team Peeta" and "Team Gale" focusing on Katniss' love life, sometimes to the exclusion of everything else.

But Katniss Everdeen—like a variety of her literary predecessors—is far more than a vertex on some love triangle. She is interesting and flawed and completely three-dimensional all on her own. She's a sister, a daughter, a friend, a hero, and—above all—a *survivor*. She's defined by her compassion, her loyalty, and her perseverance, and those are all traits she has independent of the boys.

I'm not Team Gale or Team Peeta. I'm Team Katniss, and in the next few pages, we're going to take a closer look at her character and explore the idea that the core story in the Hunger Games trilogy has less to do with who Katniss ends up with and more to do with who she *is*—because sometimes, in books and in life, it's not about the romance.

Sometimes, it's about the girl.

Meet Katniss Everdeen

Ask anyone who's ever met her—Katniss Everdeen is a hard person to know. She has one of the most recognizable faces in her entire world, but the vast majority of Panem knows very little about the *real* Katniss. To the viewers of the Games, she's the object of Peeta's affection and then a star-crossed lover herself. Later, she's the Mockingjay, the face of the rebellion, and ultimately, as far as the outside world is concerned, a broken shell of a girl pushed to the edge of insanity and beyond. Sometimes Katniss dons these masks willingly; sometimes they are thrust upon her. But one thing is certain—unlike the Careers, the flighty members of her prep team, or many of the Capitol's citizens, Katniss has no desire to be famous.

She has no desire to be known.

Whether it's with the viewers of the Games, the revolutionaries, or the townspeople in District 12, Katniss is the type to keep her distance, a fact she readily admits to in the first chapter of book one, saying that over time, she has learned to "hold [her] tongue and to turn [her] features into an indifferent mask so that no one could ever read [her] thoughts." Katniss keeps her private thoughts private and keeps most of the world at least an arm's length away. Next to Gale, Katniss' closest friend before the reaping is a girl she barely speaks to. In fact, when describing her friendship with Madge, Katniss suggests that the two of them get along primarily because they both just keep to themselves.

Clearly, this pre-reaping Katniss identifies as a loner, never getting too close to other people, never expecting too much of them so that she is never disappointed. Similarly, the people in District 12 seem content to let Katniss keep them at bay. Other than her family, Gale, and in his own adore-her-from-afar way, Peeta, there don't appear to be people lining up to know Katniss Everdeen. Even the family cat keeps his distance when she feeds him—to the point that Katniss remarks that "entrails" and "no hissing" are the closest she and Buttercup can come to love. The same could be said of Katniss' relationship with everyone from the baker to the Peacemakers who buy her contraband prey—right up until the moment she takes Prim's place at the reaping.

Standing up on the stage after she takes Prim's place, Katniss notes that it is as if a switch has been flipped, and all of a sudden, she has "become someone precious" to people who have never seemed to care about her one way or another, people who don't really know her, except through that one selfless act. As she realizes this, Katniss—in typical Katniss fashion—schools her face to be devoid of emotion, refusing to let the rest of the world see her tears, and this reluctance to give the Games' viewers anything real continues throughout the series. Our heroine's initial reaction to Haymitch telling her to make the audience feel like they know her is to explode, arguing that the Capitol has already taken away her future and that she doesn't owe them anything else. When Katniss does eventually give viewers a tiny glimpse of her love for Prim during her first pre-Games interview with Caesar Flickerman, even this revelation lays our heroine as bare as if she'd been asked to undress on camera.

Throughout the series, Katniss wears many masks—and a large part of the reason she slips into them so easily is that being the Mockingjay, or the giggling girl twirling around in her dress, or the lunatic who killed President Coin, is easier than letting people in and being herself. It's occurred to me—more than once—that maybe Katniss isn't just a hard person to know; maybe she's a hard *character* to know, too, even for those of us who are inside her head. Maybe that's why there's a tendency for readers to fall into the same trap as the viewers in the Capitol and to look for an easy answer, a handy label like "girl in love" or some kind of either/or question that will tell us exactly who Katniss Everdeen is.

Maybe, for a lot of readers, that question is *Peeta or Gale?*

Who am I?

I think there are two reasons that Katniss is a hard character for us, as readers, to wrap our minds around. The first is that Katniss isn't the kind of hero we're used to seeing in fiction. She reacts more than she acts, she doesn't want to be a leader, and by the end of *Mockingjay*, she hasn't come into her own or risen like a phoenix from the ashes for some triumphant moment that gives us a sense of satisfaction with how far our protagonist has come. She's not a Buffy. She's not a Bella. She limps across the finish line when we're used to seeing heroes racing; she eases into a quiet, steady love instead of falling fast and hard.

As much as Katniss holds herself apart from the people in her own world, she doesn't fit easily in with the canon of literary heroines either. But in addition to not fitting the mold, Katniss can be even more difficult for readers to know because though the books are told in first person, Katniss has strikingly little self-awareness. We have to work to figure Katniss out, because as often as not, *Katniss* doesn't know who she is, what she feels, or the kind of influence she wields over other people.

Peeta points this cluelessness out to Haymitch after Katniss' first interview in *The Hunger Games*, but even hearing him say that she has no idea what kind of effect she has on people, Katniss seems fully oblivious to what Peeta is talking about. She spends most of the trilogy completely unsure of her own romantic feelings, but she's equally in the dark about everything from the kind of person she is and the kind of person she wants to be to the influence she wields as the Mockingjay. Consider a moment shortly after the reaping when Katniss is told that people admire her spirit. She seems perplexed, saying "I'm not exactly sure what it means, but it suggests I'm a fighter. In a sort of brave way." The idea that a girl who volunteers for certain death to save a loved one might *not* know that she is brave is astounding, but somehow, Collins sells it absolutely.

Given that Katniss knows so little of herself, is it any wonder that she can be difficult for us to wrap our heads around, too? It seems plausible to me that one of the reasons that so many readers seem entirely invested in whether Katniss ends up with Peeta or Gale is that this seems like a more manageable question than debating the kind of person Katniss is at her core. After all, firecracker Gale and dandelion Peeta are so different from each other that it's easy to imagine that a girl who would choose Gale is a completely different person than one who would choose Peeta. When people sit around debating who Katniss should choose, maybe what they're really debating actually *is* her identity—and the romance is just a proxy for that big, hard question about the ever-changing, unaware girl on fire.

In many ways, this is a compelling idea, but I think that giving in to this line of thinking can be dangerous, because there is so much more to Katniss than her relationships with Peeta and Gale, and if this were a book about a boy who takes his brother's place at that first reaping, I wonder if we would all be sitting around talking about who he should be with, rather than who we think he should be. Katniss herself seems to resent the idea that her entire personality boils down to a romantic decision—in *Catching Fire*, she feels sickened when Haymitch tells her that she'll never be able to do anything but live "happily ever after" with Peeta. She hardens herself against the very idea of marriage until she "recoil[s] at even the suggestion of marriage or a family" (*Catching Fire*). And in *Mockingjay*, in the aftermath of Prim's death, when Katniss goes to Haymitch for help and he greets her by asking if she's having more "boy trouble," she is devastated that this is what he thinks of her, cut to her core that while her entire life is imploding, the closest thing she has to a father acts like her single biggest dilemma is deciding who she loves.

In typical Katniss style, she states that she is unsure why Haymitch's words hurt her so much, but I have my own theory, one that says that Katniss knows that the world—and many of the trilogy's readers—reduce her to that one thing—romance—and that she expects better of those who know her best.

Like Haymitch.

And—if we've taken the time as readers to dig deep enough—like us.

The Symbolic Katniss

Even though I've already argued that Katniss uses the masks she wears to keep other people at bay, I think at least one of those masks is a good to place to start when looking for clues about the girl underneath. Long before District 13 asks Katniss to officially take up the mantle of Mockingjay, she identifies with the animal in question on her own. She sings, they sing back. They're a product of the Capitol, and even before our heroine steps foot in the arena, so is she. Mockingjays are adaptive, and, as Katniss notes, the Capitol severely underestimated the species' desire to survive.

At the end of *Catching Fire*, in a daze from having been violently extracted from the arena, Katniss makes what is perhaps the strongest statement of her own identity in the entire series: "The bird, the pin, the song, the berries, the watch, the cracker, the dress that burst into flames. I am the mockingjay. The one that survived despite the Capitol's plans. The symbol of the rebellion." It seems that Katniss' entire life—or at the very least, her life since she took Prim's place at the reaping—has been leading to this, as her tiny acts of bravery and compassion and cunning spark a revolution. For once, Katniss is aware of exactly what she symbolizes and how her actions have led to this moment—and yet, Katniss herself is no more of a rebel than an actual mockingjay, an animal who never thought of thwarting the Capitol and merely wanted to survive.

Katniss is, at her core, a survivor—a fact that is reinforced by her very name. In stark contrast to Prim and Rue, who were both named after pretty, delicate flowers, Katniss was named after a root—one that can be eaten like a potato, leading her father to have once commented that as long as Katniss could find herself, she'd never starve (ironic, given that Katniss spends much of the series trying to figure out who exactly she is). It's a practical name: no frills, no fuss, all about the bottom line.

Survival.

Whether she's "Katniss" or "the Mockingjay," it's all right there in the name: Katniss is the kind of person who does what she needs to do to survive. Her other dominant character-istic—the one other thing that's important to her—should be obvious, given that she entered the Hunger Games voluntarily to save Prim.

Family.

To this end, I'd argue that there might be a better symbol for Katniss than the mockingjay or the potato-like plant after which she was named, one that shows up like clockwork in every book of the trilogy, tracing Katniss' path as she goes.

Buttercup.

I know that it might seem crazy to some people that I think you can get a better sense Katniss' character by looking at The Cat Who Refuses To Die than by debating the relative merits of Peeta versus Gale, but at the end of the day, if I had to pick a "team" (other than Team Katniss, of course), I would pick Team Buttercup. Not because I don't love Peeta (I do) or Gale (also do), but because I can't help looking at that beat-up old cat, who arrived at the Everdeen household as a scrawny little kitten, and thinking about how very much like Katniss he is. Standoffish. Protective. A creature who, against all odds, survives.

Gale may be the one who promises to protect Prim when Katniss leaves for the Games, but Buttercup is the one she trusts to watch over her little sister—to comfort her when she cries, to love her. Other than the fact that Buttercup's a great hunter and has a less-than-approachable personality, his two most defining characteristics are that he survives things a cat has no business surviving and that he loves Prim.

Sound familiar?

Throughout the trilogy, these same two characteristics are the ones that drive Katniss' actions the most. She is focused, sometimes to the exclusion of everything else, on finding a way to survive and protecting the people she considers family so that they may do the same. The importance Katniss puts on survival and family seems obvious, not just to us as readers, but to the handful of people who actually know Katniss. Peeta and Gale agree that Katniss will ultimately choose whoever she can't survive without, and even President Snow hits the nail on the head, saying, "Any girl who goes to such lengths to preserve her life isn't going to be interested in throwing it away" (*Catching Fire*). Significantly, however, President Snow doesn't end his appraisal of Katniss with that statement about her will to survive; in a threatening tone, he adds on, "And then there's her family to think of," pinpointing her second major priority as well. Katniss is a survivor, and she lives to protect those she loves. Snow knows exactly how to threaten her, because—like the rest of the major players in the series—he knows exactly what our heroine's priorities are.

But what is significantly less obvious—and what I think accounts for many of the character developments we see in *Mockingjay* (and the fact that Katniss fails to go suddenly Buffy and start kicking ass left and right)—is the fact that together, these two driving forces—the ability to survive and an intense love for people who might not—can only lead one place when you put Katniss in any kind of war. Suffice to say, it's not a happy place, and to really understand it—and the girl—you have to take a step back and think about how Katniss views family and what it means to her to survive.

Survivor

For Katniss, the name of the game has always been survival. At the age of eleven, with her father dead and her mother falling to pieces, Katniss had to make a choice, and she chose to set aside her own grief and fight for her family and for herself. To Katniss, whose mother "went away" and became an emotional invalid after her father's death, this must have seemed like an either/or situation: you can either grieve for your lost loved ones or you can plow on; you can love and risk being decimated, or you can survive.

It's little wonder, then, that in Katniss' mind romance was something she "never had the time or use for" (*Hunger Games*) and that when circumstances forced her to start thinking of love, it was always, always tied in her mind to survival. When Gale asks Katniss to go away with him at the beginning of the first book, she turns him down and only later begins to wonder whether the invitation was a practical means of increasing their chances of survival or whether it was something more. Shortly thereafter, when comparing her feelings about Peeta to her feelings about Gale, Katniss explicitly ties romance and survival together, saying, "Gale and I were thrown together by a mutual need to survive. Peeta and I know the other's survival means our death. How do you sidestep that?"

Romance and survival, survival and romance.

For Katniss, they have always gone hand in hand. And yet, when she overhears Gale telling Peeta that her romantic choice will ultimately come down to who she can't survive without,

Katniss is completely thrown and hurt that Gale sees her as being so cold and passionless. She wonders if Gale is right, and if that makes her selfish or less of a person—but what Katniss not-so-shockingly doesn't seem to realize about herself is that she absolutely, one hundred percent *isn't* the kind of person who prizes her survival above all else.

There is at least one thing that matters to her more.

Katniss comments in *Catching Fire* that if she had been older when her father died, she might well have ended up prostituting herself to the Peacekeepers to keep Prim fed. During the Quarter Quell, she goes in with the full intention of dying, so that Peeta might live. Neither of those actions is the work of a girl with a cold heart and a Machiavellian approach to survival. Katniss throws herself in front of bullets as often as she dodges them—because she would rather die for the people she loves than see them hurt.

Daughter, Sister, Mother, Friend

If anyone doubts that Katniss is more driven by family than anything else—including romance—all you have to do is look at the role that Prim plays in almost every major turning point in the series. For a character who exists primarily off-screen, she's instrumental in nearly everything Katniss does. She's the impetus for Katniss volunteering for the Games. In *Catching Fire*, she's the reason Katniss considers taking to the woods and the reason she decides not to—if her job is to protect Prim, she's already failed, because the Capitol has been hurting her little sister since the day she was born. In *Mockingjay*, Prim is the first one who spells out for Katniss exactly how much power she has as the Mockingjay, and Prim's death kicks off

the final act of the book, cutting off one vertex of the Katniss/
Peeta/Gale love triangle as viciously as a bomb can blow off a
leg. Prim is the first character, other than Katniss, to appear in
the books, and Katniss' very first action on the very first page
is to reach for her and come up empty-handed.

If that's not foreshadowing, I don't know what is.

But although Katniss identifies Prim as "the only person in
the world I'm certain I love" (*Hunger Games*), throughout the
course of the series, we see Katniss taking other people into her
heart.

Adopting them.

Making them family.

The most of obvious case of this is Rue. Katniss takes her in,
casts her in Prim's role, tries to protect her and fails. Rue's death,
more even than the promise Katniss made to Prim, is what drives
our heroine to devote herself to winning the Games—because the
only way to make Rue's death mean something, to make her
unforgettable, is "by winning and thereby making [herself] unforgettable." In the span of less than twenty-four hours, Katniss lets
Rue past all of her shields. She trusts her. She makes her family.

And then Rue dies.

While the little girl from District 11 is the only one, other
than Prim, who gets the word "love" out of Katniss in that first
book, even if it is in the lyrics of a song, this isn't a pattern that
holds up for long. Throughout the series, we see Katniss
bringing more and more people into her fold: Peeta and
Haymitch, Mags, Johanna and Finnick, Cinna. As focused as
Katniss is on her own family, and as much as she tries to "protect" herself from letting other people in, the number of people
the Capitol can use to hurt her just keeps growing and growing.
The number of people Katniss feels she must protect keeps getting bigger and bigger.

And the number of times she will inevitably fail becomes innumerable.

The End

Katniss is a survivor, and she's a protector. She's a person who creates family everywhere she goes and a person who loves fiercely—but she lives in a brutal world, a world in which she cannot protect the ones she loves, a world in which survival—and living without her loved ones—is more of a curse than it is a blessing.

I would like to argue that this—and not any kind of romantic decision—is what makes Katniss Everdeen the person we see at the series' end. Her drive and ability to survive and her fierce love of the family she's made are the traits that account for every single moment named in *Mockingjay* when Haymitch asks people to talk about times when they were personally affected by Katniss' actions. Ultimately, even to the other characters in the book, Katniss isn't The Girl Who Chose Peeta. She's not The Mockingjay or The Girl on Fire or The Girl Who Didn't Choose Gale.

She's a girl who survives something horrible and loses far too many people along the way.

There's an episode of *Buffy the Vampire Slayer* that I've been thinking about a lot while writing this essay. In it, Buffy sacrifices her own life to save her sister, and right before she does, she tells her sister that the hardest thing to do in the world is to live—ironic words coming from someone about to kill herself for the greater good. As I'm writing this, I just keep thinking that Katniss never gets to sacrifice herself. She doesn't get the heroic death. She survives—and that leaves her doing the hardest thing in the world: living in it once so many of the ones that she loves are gone.

The very last we see of Katniss in *Mockingjay* is an epilogue in which she's still struggling with that, even as we learn that she's come full circle and given birth to a new family. Some people probably read that epilogue and think, "Okay, so Katniss chose Peeta and they had kids. The End." I read it and think that Katniss chose to go on—again. She chose to love—again. She's scarred, but she survived—and she loves her children just as fiercely as she loved Prim.

That's who Katniss is, underneath all of the masks—and if we're picking teams, I'm on hers.

JENNIFER LYNN BARNES *is the author of seven books for young adults, including* Tattoo, Fate, *the* Squad *series, and* Raised by Wolves, *a paranormal adventure about a human girl raised by werewolves. Jen graduated from Yale University in 2006 with a degree in cognitive science and Cambridge University in 2007 with a master's in psychiatry. She's currently hard at work on a PhD.*

YOUR HEART IS A WEAPON THE SIZE OF YOUR FIST

▶

Love as a Political Act in the Hunger Games

MARY BORSELLINO

We see some really memorable weapons in the Hunger Games series. The wolf mutts with the eyes of the dead tributes in *The Hunger Games* stand out, as does Katniss' bow. There are Gale's snares, as effective at trapping people as animals, and of course the multitude of horrors contained in the Capitol's pods in *Mockingjay*. For Mary Borsellino, though, none of these even come close to the most powerful weapon in the series: love.

There's a piece of graffiti on a wall in Palestine. Over the years since it was painted, it's been photographed by scores of travelers and journalists. It reads:

Your heart is a weapon the size of your fist. Keep fighting. Keep loving.

More than bombs, fire, guns or arrows, love is the most powerful weapon in the Hunger Games. It stirs and feeds the rebellion. It saves the doomed. It destroys the bereaved. And it gives even the most devastated survivors a reason to go on.

"Love" is not synonymous with "passion". Hatred is also a passionate emotion. When I say "love" here, I mean compassion, loyalty, empathy, and the bonds of friendship, family, and romance. All these things are present in Suzanne Collins' Hunger Games series. So too are greed, selfishness, hatred, and fear. That the protagonists are able to put stock in love, even while given so many reasons to hate, is what gives the Hunger Games a note of hope despite the suffering of the characters.

The Hunger Games is part of a genre of post-apocalyptic political fiction, the best known example of which is George Orwell's *Nineteen Eighty-Four*. Suzanne Collins has said that *Nineteen Eighty-Four* is a book she reads over and over again,[1] and the Hunger Games shows a great debt to Orwell's novel and to subsequent variations on it such as the graphic novel *V for Vendetta*.

---

1. See *People* magazine double issue #116/117, August 20/27, 2010.

Both the Hunger Games and *Nineteen Eighty-Four* pit the power of hate versus the power of love. In *Nineteen Eighty-Four*, it's hate that ultimately triumphs, but the Hunger Games—which is American, as opposed to British, and so perhaps comes from a more culturally optimistic place when it comes to rebellions—ultimately insists that love is strong enough to survive through the horrors placed before it.

The Hunger Games' Katniss was a hard, calculating, distrustful person even before her time in the arenas and the war, and yet her largest decisions are always motivated by love. She volunteers for the Games in order to save Prim's life, something that is almost never done because the Capitol teaches people to put their own self-preservation before any bond of love in such a situation, even a bond as close as that between Katniss and Prim. Katniss defies this.

Suzanne Collins has explained that Katniss is "a girl who should never have existed," an unexpected outcome of a security glitch in the Capitol's regime, just like the mockingjays. She is "this girl who slips under this fence . . . and along with that goes a degree of independent thinking that is unusual in the districts."[2]

Neither of the cages the Capitol has in place—the fence, prioritizing self-preservation over love for family or friends—hold her, and by breaking out, she makes other people realize that they can too. On live television, all over Panem, she introduces a radical new idea: that it is important to care about other people; that it is the most important thing in the world.

While we're talking about television, it's important to touch on one of the strangest ways in which the Hunger Games owes a debt to *Nineteen Eighty-Four*. *Nineteen Eighty-Four* includes the

---

2. See her interview in *School Library Journal*: http://www.schoollibraryjournal.com/slj/home/885800-312/the_last_battle_with_mockingjay.html.csp.

phrase "Big Brother is watching you," which in that novel means that the state—personified by its leader, Big Brother—can see everything you do. You are never safe from its surveillance, and all treason will be found out.

These days, of course, "Big Brother" means something completely different, as it is the name of one of the first of the wildly popular shows in the reality television genre. In *Big Brother*, a group of people are thrown together in a closed environment and watched by audiences at home. Big Brother is watching them, and we are watching *Big Brother*.

President Snow, in controlling the districts via the Hunger Games, is both Big Brothers at once: the dictator and the reality television producer. The Hunger Games series very consciously plays with the fact that it follows not only Orwell's novel, but also the entertainment revolution it inadvertantly spawned.

In *Nineteen Eighty-Four* there is another equivalent to President Snow, a character named O'Brien who, in describing how his government has achieved such total power over people, also neatly sums up the Capitol's intentions:

We have cut the links between child and parent, and between man and man, and between man and woman.

This is what makes Katniss' self-sacrifice for Prim such a powerful act. If the Capitol had really succeeded at severing those links, then it would have been Primrose Everdeen who went into the arena, not her older sister, wouldn't it?

And there is a love story in *Nineteen Eighty-Four*, just as there is one in the Hunger Games. In *Nineteen Eighty-Four*, it is between a man named Winston and a woman named Julia. Like Peeta in *Mockingjay*, Winston and Julia are punished for their rebellion by being tortured in specific ways that make them hate the person they were once in love with. Like Katniss, their wills are finally broken when they are presented with what, to them, is the worst thing in the world. (The worst thing for Katniss was losing Prim, but for Winston it is much more banal: he has a phobia of rats, and is threatened with being eaten by them. Julia's worst fear is never revealed to the reader.)

When the two love stories are compared, you can see much of Winston and Julia in the way Suzanne Collins has written Peeta and Katniss' story, and in just how important and powerful the romance Peeta and Katniss put on for the cameras through the first two novels of the trilogy is in stoking the flames of the rebellion.

In *Nineteen Eighty-Four*, Winston and Julia's love story starts when Julia slips Winston a piece of paper as they bump into one another one day.

> Whatever was written on the paper, it must have some kind of political meaning. . . . He flattened it out. On it was written, in a large unformed handwriting: I LOVE YOU.

If that sounds like a bait-and-switch—he expected something political, but really she's in love with him!—think again. Love when there isn't supposed to be love is a hugely subversive political act. If it weren't, there wouldn't be protest marches in countries all over the world demanding same-sex marriage. It was illegal until 1967 for black and white people to marry one another in some parts of the USA. A 2007 survey found that more than half of the Jewish people in Israel believed intermarriage between Jewish females and Arab males was equivalent to national treason.

When the love you feel is against the laws of those in control, then love is a political act. It's true in the real world, true in *Nineteen Eighty-Four*, and true in the Hunger Games.

When Katniss and Peeta make as if to kill themselves rather than one another at the end of the first Games, it is seen by President Snow as dangerous because it could be interpreted as an act of rebellion. In *Catching Fire*, he demands that Katniss convince the districts that she acted out of love for Peeta, not out of defiance against the Capitol. As far as Snow can see, her actions are either/or—either Katniss looks like a rebel or she looks like a girl in love; her motivation can only be one or the other.

What President Snow never understands is that choosing love over survival is the ultimate act of defiance Katniss can make. It's not one or the other; the love and rebellion are one in the same.

The Capitol teaches almost everyone to see the tributes as less than human: when Katniss is first being styled by her prep team, they wax and scrub her and then declare happily that she looks almost like a person. Before that, when Katniss says good-bye to Gale, he tells her that killing the other tributes won't be any different to killing animals in the woods. When President Snow's scientists hijack Peeta and make him think that Katniss is a mutt it is only another example of the Capitol's commitment to dehumanization.

But Katniss doesn't accept that. She sees the value in human life, even as she is forced into becoming a killer and soldier. She teams up with Rue in the arena, rather than simply killing the little girl and taking out some of her competition. When Rue dies, Katniss sings to her, and covers her with flowers.

The effect of this tiny, humanizing act—singing to a dying child—has immediate and far reaching consequences. Rue's district sends Katniss bread. Rue's fellow tribute spares her life when they face off later in the Games. In *Catching Fire*, it's Rue's song that the district whistles to Katniss to show their support for her, and in *Mockingjay* Boggs offers Katniss' singing as a moment when he was touched by her.

Do you begin to see what President Snow couldn't?

Love, like fire, is catching.

Katniss, going along with Snow's plan to make the romance with Peeta seem to be the cause of her actions, can't see it either. But with every interview and appearance, she declares herself loyal to something other than the Capitol. And love has already proved to be more powerful than the Capitol, because both of District 12's tributes have survived the Games.

Another post-apocalyptic political story of recent years was the graphic novel, and subsequent film, *V for Vendetta*. It, like the Hunger Games, is the story of the figurehead of a rebellion, and of a teenage girl, Evie. It, too, shows clear echoes of *Nineteen Eighty-Four* in its storytelling.

When Evie is captured by the police and taken to jail, she finds a letter hidden in her cell. It was from an earlier prisoner, Valerie, and tells the story of Valerie's life. Valerie was gay, rounded up and put to death in a concentration camp. In the letter left behind, she wrote:

> Our integrity sells for so little, but it is all we really have. It is the very last inch of us. . . . An inch, it is small and it is fragile, but it is the only thing in the world worth having. We must never lose it or give it away. We must never let them take it from us. . . . what I hope most of all is that you understand what I mean when I tell you that even though I do not know you, and even though I may never meet you, laugh with you, cry with you, or kiss you. I love you. With all my heart, I love you.

Valerie died because of who she loved, but her love is stronger than the hate that executed her. It survives her death, waiting patiently in the cell until Evie comes and finds it later.

Julia and Winston's love doesn't survive the things that they are put through when they are captured—the tortures hijack that last inch of them. When they see each other again, as broken and hijacked as Peeta becomes in *Mockingjay*, Winston thinks of an old song lyric:

> *Under the spreading chestnut tree*
> *I sold you and you sold me.*

The last time Katniss sees Peeta in the war, before trying to infiltrate Snow's mansion and instead witnessing the violent and horrific death of her sister, she imagines Gale being taken by Peacekeepers and Peeta being forced to take the nightlock poison. She then thinks of "The Hanging Tree" song:

> *Are you, are you*
> *Coming to the tree*

Combined, the two songs become a question posed to Peeta and Katniss: will fear, torture, hate, lust for power, and the desire for self-preservation ultimately prove to be so strong that even lovers would betray each other? Are they coming to the chestnut tree, where they will sell each other out?

The Hunger Games, however, declare that no, love *does* conquer hate, even in circumstances as dire as Katniss and Peeta's. Their love survives what Winston and Julia's cannot.

Katniss and Peeta both have moments of suicidal despair in *Mockingjay*. Peeta is tortured until he can't even remember what his favorite color is, much less whether or not he loves Katniss.

Katniss loses Prim, the sister she loves more than her own life. They are broken as absolutely as Julia and Winston are broken.

But Katniss is driven by love and compassion, even when the thing she loves most in the world is dead. When President Coin asks the surviving tributes whether another Hunger Games should be held, Katniss understands that Coin is no different, in the end, than Snow. In order to ensure herself an opportunity to assassinate Coin, Katniss gives a vote of yes to the new round of Games, and says that she does so "for Prim."

The explanation seems, on the surface, to be one of vengeance: for Prim's death, Katniss wants to see the children of the Capitol suffer in the same way. But in reality her motivation is self-sacrifice: Katniss began her journey when she put her own life in danger for Prim, for a child who would otherwise have died in the arena. Expecting to die after the assassination, Katniss once again places the life of children bound for the arena before her own by killing the woman who would have reinstated the Games. And Katniss does so out of love—she does it for Prim, even if Prim is already dead.

Katniss remains true, even in the face of crushing loss and the prospect of her own death, to an ideal that Winston has in *Nineteen Eighty-Four* but is ultimately unable to uphold himself: "the object was not to stay alive but to stay human." Katniss retains that last inch of integrity and love that Valerie of *V for Vendetta* prized above life.

This is not to say that the power of love is always a triumphant force in the Hunger Games. Katniss' mother is a skilled healer who can face terrible injury and illness without flinching, but losing her husband almost killed her and, because she was incapable of caring for them in her depressed state, almost killed her daughters as well. Prim's death hits her so hard that she can not be there for Katniss in the aftermath.

Love is the greatest strength any of the characters have going for them, but is also their greatest weakness. President Snow was able to coerce Finnick into sexual slavery by threatening to hurt those that Finnick loved if he didn't comply.

Yet the alternative—to have nobody you love—is infinitely worse than being made vulnerable by love. Johanna Mason explains in *Catching Fire* that there is nobody left whom she loves, and that this renders the jabberjays in the arena unable to hurt her through mimicking screams, though her meltdown during training in *Mockingjay* shows that even someone who loves nobody can still be wounded terribly by the Capitol.

When Peeta and Katniss are each wounded, just as deeply as Johanna, they have the other there to help them on the slow and rocky path to recovery. Johanna is no less damaged for her lack of love, but she doesn't have anyone to help her back afterwards.

Like Johanna, neither Snow nor Coin indicate at any point in the Hunger Games that there is anyone or any thing that they themselves love. But both think that they understand what a powerful force love is, and both do their best to wield this power for their own evil ends.

In each case, however, their efforts backfire: by making Katniss emphasize her love story in *Catching Fire*, Snow does more to incite the rebellion against his Capitol than Katniss could have achieved on her own. And Coin, in attempting to reinstate the Hunger Games as a method of offering revenge to the districts, seals the death warrant on her regime and her self. The woman who views marriage as a reassignment of living quarters cannot anticipate the steadfast core of Katniss' compassion. She nor Snow ever really understand love at all.

So what can we take from the stories of Winston and Julia, of Valerie, of Katniss and Peeta? Why does George Orwell end his love story with the lovers broken and defeated? Why does writer Alan Moore kill off the defiant Valerie? And, with these grim precedents in place, why does Suzanne Collins then decide to give Katniss and Peeta a fragile, scarred, but undeniably happy ending?

The answer may come from the connection Peeta and Katniss share to the land of District 12. The first time Katniss sees Peeta again, he is gardening, and it is the fearlessness Katniss feels in the wild that allowed her to survive her first trip to the Arena. Katniss and Peeta are both linked to the natural world, and in the natural world even the worst of winters is followed by a spring.

The epilogue of *Mockingjay* shows Katniss watching her children play in the Meadow, now green and lush once again. New life grows, even in graveyards. Rue's funeral song is able to become a child's simple tune once more. There are losses to mourn, but also children to love: Prim and her mother have both left Katniss forever, a discarded knitting basket remaining as a reminder, but Greasy Sae's granddaughter is there to take the wool instead.

Katniss and Peeta are both terribly scarred, physically and psychologically, by their experiences in the arenas and the war. But they are able to go on, and survive the pain. Katniss describes the way she copes with her moments of terror and pain: "I make a list in my head of every act of goodness I've seen someone do."

Katniss Everdeen can survive her darkness because she understands the same truth that's expressed in that graffiti in Palestine. Her heart is a weapon, and the way to keep fighting against all the horror and cruelty of the world is to wield that weapon. To keep loving.

MARY BORSELLINO *is a writer who lives in Melbourne, Australia. Her latest books are the acclaimed Wolf House series. Her website is http://www.maryborsellino.com and her email is mizmary@gmail.com. She likes punk rock, cups of tea, and clever people. She cried really hard at the end of* Mockingjay.

SMOKE AND MIRRORS

▶

Reality vs. Unreality in the Hunger Games

ELIZABETH M. REES

Imagine living in a world where you can't trust anyone—not your neighbors, not your friends—and you're never alone or safe—not in the woods, not in your home, not at your job. Or just think about what it would be like to grow up in Panem. In such a world, the only way to survive is by learning to see through the deceptions that surround you and figure out how to use them to your own advantage. Here, Elizabeth M. Rees takes us through the layers of smoke and mirrors in the Hunger Games series and the challenges Katniss faces in her pursuit of truth.

smoke and mirrors: cover-up; something that is intended to draw attention away from something else that somebody would prefer remain unnoticed

—Encarta World English Dictionary

smoke and mirrors: irrelevant or misleading information serving to obscure the truth of a situation

—Collins English Dictionary

When I was a kid my favorite game was "Let's Pretend." Every child plays one version or another. You create a world for a day, or an afternoon, complete with rules, with adventures, with tragedies and silly happenings, everything from tea parties to out-and-out galactic warfare. But then your mom calls you in for dinner, or to do chores or homework, and game time ends. Poof! The pretend world evaporates into thin air, never to exist in exactly the same way again.

But what if it never vanished? What if all that pretense, that make-believe, wasn't imaginary at all? What if your whole world, day-in and day-out, was made up of pretense, lies, and deceit? What if your life or your death depended on rules that change on a whim? What if to survive at all, you too have to learn to play a game of smoke and mirrors—to master a game constructed of lies, one that you can never control?

Katniss Everdeen, in Suzanne Collins' Hunger Games series, is forced to do just that. Even as Katniss is engulfed in ever more vicious treachery, sinister tricks, and heartbreaking betrayals, her hero's task is to penetrate the smoke and mirrors that delude herself and others until she can at last distinguish the real from the unreal, both in her own life and in Panem.

Homeschooled in Deception

At the beginning of the first book we are introduced to the convolutions of survival in Panem through Katniss' daily struggles in District 12. The government masquerades as some kind of democracy: it does sport a president, albeit one with dictatorial powers.[1] In Big Brother style, the Capitol suppresses any kind of dissent, behind the guise, of course, of "protecting" its citizens. Services that could ease the difficult lives of the residents are meted out according to each district's usefulness to the Capitol (electricity is sporadic, at least in the least-favored districts). Within each district resources are never fairly distributed in the markets frequented by the general public. Fuel and food are doled out in amounts that barely sustain the populace. Only the elite of each district, and mainly of the Capitol, benefit from the grueling labor of Panem's citizens.

The government's heavy hand hovers over the districts as it metes out draconian punishment for the smallest of offenses: illegal hunting merits a public whipping and/or time in the stocks, and even casual comments against the government lead to death—or to life—as an Avox, rendered mute and forced to

---

1. Some kind of campaign or political process is implied in *Mockingjay*, where Coin first tries to get Katniss killed off by Peeta—deflecting any blame away from herself—to thwart any attempt by Katniss to become president after Snow, or to keep her from supporting any rival of Coin's.

live a life of slavery serving the wealthy denizens of the Capitol. To police its citizens the Capitol eavesdrops: during the first rebellion, it used muttations like the jabberjays, which could mimic human speech, to parrot back to the authorities everything they heard. Since then the government has employed alternate means mysterious to Katniss, but which we later learn include phone tapping.[2] To insure that no one forgets the price of an uprising all of Panem is held in thrall by the Games and the terrible ritual of the reaping, where the child-tributes are ripped from their homes and families in order to kill each other.

Survival in such circumstances is difficult at best, but after Katniss' father dies in a mining accident, survival for her and her family means constant negotiation of a maze of lies, pretense, and deception. The alternative: death by starvation, or an even worse fate than death. Rendered totally dysfunctional by grief, their mother couldn't care for her children's most basic needs, but if they look too disheveled, or grow weak and sick, Prim and Katniss would be taken by Peacekeepers to the Seam's community home—an institution masquerading as a refuge. Community home kids arrive at Katniss' school black and blue and battered.[3] Katniss refuses to let Prim suffer this fate. But she has no "legal" recourse to stop the downward spiral of their existence. All she has are the forbidden hunting skills her father taught her. Though only eleven at the time, she braves the predator-filled wilderness beyond the fenced-in borders and retrieves

---

2. When Snow confronts Katniss with knowledge that she disappears "into the woods with him each Sunday," she has no idea how he knows this (*Catching Fire*). Are they being tracked by people, cameras?

3. "I'd grown up seeing those home kids at school. The sadness, the marks of angry hands on their faces, the hopelessness that curled their shoulders forward" (*The Hunger Games*).

her bow and arrow to provide her first meager meal for her family.

The electrified perimeter fence Katniss breaches to reach the forest serves a dual purpose: it keeps dangerous predators out, but it also keeps residents in. Katniss, like most residents of the Seam, knows the fence is a sham. Current hasn't run through it for years. Yet everyone pretends the fence is operational. That touching it will kill you. It's also in need of mending, which is what allows Katniss to crawl underneath.

The defunct fence is one reason Katniss and Gale can ignore laws with impunity while feeding their families and bartering their daily catch for needed goods in the Hob, the District's informal trading and black market hub. The other reason is the district's powers-that-be, who with a wink and a nod condone not only the black market machine itself but also Katniss and Gale's contribution to keeping it well-oiled and functioning. The Mayor is Katniss' best customer for strawberries harvested beyond the fence. Even the Capitol's Peacekeepers enjoy the illegal fare.

Both the thriving black market and the dysfunctional perimeter fence benefit everyone who lives in the Seam—rich or poor. The black market allows those who are better off access to delicacies available only to the Capitol's residents and lets enterprising poor like Katniss survive. To acknowledge the fence is broken or that illicit trading is going on is to invite a crackdown from the Capitol, and District 12 is used to being left alone.

District 12 is so impoverished that until Katniss' and Peeta's return as victors, the Capitol has little interest in the local law enforcement. The residents are too weak and underfed to create much trouble—as long as the Seam continues to produce enough coal to fuel Panem's energy needs, the Capitol is content to ignore it.

Of course, taking advantage of that neglect still requires Katniss to play her own game of Let's Pretend—to constantly conjure up her own version of smoke and mirrors. She must go to the Mayor's backdoor to sell her strawberries because she can't afford "to be seen" doing so, even though the Mayor himself is her customer. She trades the meat she gets with Peacekeepers, but she must stow her bow and arrow in a hollow log inside the forest, much as her father did. Being caught with weapons is a capital offense in Panem. So Katniss adheres to the letter of the law, careful never to be seen with a weapon, even though her customers know she must use one to hunt.

Katniss has also mastered the art of masquerade, at least in terms of her feelings. To keep her family alive and safe, Katniss continually masks her resentment toward the unjust system that keeps everyone hungry, weak, and dependent on the corrupt Capitol. Keenly aware of the long arm of the Capitol, never knowing who is listening to what she, or Prim, or Gale might say in an unguarded moment, Katniss harbors a deep anger and resentment toward the Capitol. The very existence of the reaping further fuels the fire in her belly. But it is a fire she has learned to keep hidden. To express any disapproval of government policies is a death sentence. Whether she hunts or not, whether she is angry or not, doesn't matter. What is important is how her actions appear.

By the day of the reaping, Katniss has become a grade-A student of deceit. On her home turf she has first hand experience of the Capitol's sleight of hand: the electrified fence with no current, the Peacekeepers who pretend not to know she owns weapons, the horrors inside the supposed refuge of the Community Home. Nothing is ever what it seems. And not only has she learned to see through the Capitol's trickery and find which rules can be bent, even broken without repercussions, she has mastered the skills to take advantage of that vision. Her life in

District 12 has been a kind of boot camp, or prep school, training her not just with the physical skills of a hunter, but also teaching her to be able to mask her feelings, to live inside a necessary lie—just to survive.

So in many ways Katniss is well prepared for the Games. The skills that allow her to hunt successfully for food can be easily if not comfortably applied to killing her fellow tributes. And she intuits immediately that a tribute who—even at the reapings— seems weak and fearful, like a frightened rabbit or deer, will go down fast in the arena. No sponsors will ever come to a weakling's rescue. Thus, standing in front of the crowds at the reaping, she both knows to and is able to feign boredom, her face betraying none of the emotions roiling inside her.

But even as she first boards the train that will take her to the Capitol Katniss is brutally aware that she has to ramp up her survival tactics—fast! No one can be trusted—not even the boy whose one kind gesture when they were children stirred the embers of her flickering instinct to survive. She is determined never to drop her guard; she must remain as wary as she did while hunting—wary now just not of animal predators but of everything and every person she encounters before and during the Games.

The Arena: A Maze of Tricks and Traps

Even before Katniss reaches the Capitol, we realize there are ways in which she is not at all prepared for the Games. District 12 has been her training ground, yes, but nothing in Katniss' previous experience can prepare her for the calculated, psychologically brutal nature of the Gamemakers' tricks and traps or the kinds of deceptions necessary to survive during the Games, and after them. Ironically it's in the arenas of the Games themselves—as well as on *Mockingjay*'s urban battleground—that the dark art of smoke and mirrors reach a savage perfection.

Katniss is good at figuring out rules and how to get around them, and these skills help her discern the complex patterns the Gamemakers wove into the Games. Certain sections of the arena, she realizes, present specific threats. This is even more apparent in *Catching Fire*, where the arena's horrors are timed to be released at specific hours in specific predictable quadrants—jabberjays, acid fog, killer monkeys. Katniss also understands the Gamemakers' need to keep the TV audience entertained. A day with no kills, no action, might bore the audience and so always leads to a ramping up of challenges in the arena.

These are all things Katniss can learn and then predict. But what makes the Games so treacherous is that even the things that should be predictable frequently aren't—and being caught unaware, by another tribute or by one of the Gamemakers' toys, can lead to death. After all, these "toys" are specifically designed to catch tributes unaware.

Snares—physical and psychological—play crucial roles in Collins' trilogy. Snares are by nature hidden: a passive weapon, they are usually some kind of net or wire that is camouflaged, often cleverly buried in leaf litter, to trap unsuspecting game so that they may be more easily killed later. Snares are considered fair play for the hunter, and the first ones the reader encounters seem innocuous enough—as long as you aren't a rabbit or squirrel caught in one of Gale's ingenious traps. But in the arena the victims are not rabbits, but humans. Ill-fated Rue, certainly one of the most compelling characters in the series, meets her death in *The Hunger Games* when she is caught in a net and then speared like a helpless rabbit or fawn.

Catching Fire extends the concept of snares with Beetee's masterful, rather complicated use of wire to electrify the area of the jungle near the Cornucopia, and thus kill two of the other tributes. And the urban battleground of *Mockingjay* is literally a minefield of snares—fiendish pods that lay in wait for passersby and that incorporate the Capitol's weapons, either familiar ones from the arena games or new, even more nefarious creations.

But the series' most memorable snare of all doesn't need a net. In a tried and true terrorist device borrowed from our world, bombs hidden in parachutes are dropped from a hovercraft with the Capitol insignia onto a group of children outside of Snow's mansion. Parachutes are familiar to the kids from watching the Games: they deliver presents, good things. But these parachutes are deadly, exploding when the children grab them. And as rebel medics, horrified Capitol Peacekeepers, and citizens rush in to help, a second fiery bomb explodes, maiming and killing the would-be rescuers.

This brilliant amoral snare, a more complex, heinous version of one of Gale and Beetee's traps, works because it understands the psychology of its targets and uses that understanding to undo them. Reluctantly Katniss comes to believe the exploding parachutes are the work of the rebellion. But everyone else remains convinced the Capitol is responsible for the unconscionable devastation; after all, the weapon bears all the hallmarks of Snow and company's brutally effective mind games

Mutts—short for "muttations," the foul genetic products of the Capitol's continued quest for means to subdue Panem's citizens—are another of the Gamemakers' favorite weapons. In the first book, mutts resembling huge wolves attack Katniss, Peeta, and Cato at the Cornucopia. But it is when Katniss looks into the beasts' eyes that the true horror of the mutts is revealed: Rue, Foxface, all the dead tributes, allies and foes alike, stare out at her. In case she is in doubt she sees the number eleven on the collar circling the neck of the one whose eyes belong to District 11's tribute, Rue. Jabberjays are manipulated to mimic the agonized cries of people dear to the tributes, and in the second Games, they practically drive Katniss and Finnick to suicide. Then there are the tracker jackers, armed with hallucinogenic venom. Katniss herself is stung during the first Games and, even with a mild dose, experiences mind-bending apparitions. One of her ghoulish visions shows "ants crawl[ing] out of the blisters on my hands." She later she tells us that the "nature of [the] venom . . . target[s] the place where fear lives in your brain" (*The Hunger Games*). And of course it is tracker jacker venom that President Snow uses on Peeta to alter his memories of Katniss.

What all these weapons have in common is that, at their core, they are about deception. The snares rely on deception to lure their victims in, whether they appear to be safe, solid ground (but turn out to be a net) or a parachuted care package (but turn out to be a bomb). The jabberjays and the wolf mutts that attack Katniss and Peeta at the end of the first Games are also effective only through deception: it's the tributes' belief that they are hearing their loved ones being tortured (or that the jabberjays are repeating their loved ones' screams) and Katniss and Peeta's initial belief that they are seeing the dead tributes looking through the mutts' eyes that makes them truly horrific. And deception is at the very heart of the tracker jackers' effectiveness; their venom's power is in rendering victims unable to tell what is real from what is not.

After the initial surprise, Katniss is able to cope with the deceptions used against her by the Gamemakers. What challenges Katniss most are the psychological deceptions she must take part in to survive—the costumes, the interviews, but in particular, the deception involving Peeta. It takes all her willpower to go along with Haymitch's strategy, spelled out during their first meal in the Training Center, that she and Peeta are to feign friendship. Katniss is comfortable play-acting the absence of emotion, but pretending that she and Peeta are linked emotionally is repugnant to her. It's an out-and-out lie, but, like many others in Katniss' odyssey, one she must embrace. Katniss agrees to it, but she does so with great skepticism. Eventually she will have to kill Peeta, or he'll have to kill her. Her promise to Prim makes it perfectly clear to her who is going to kill whom in the end. So what is the purpose in pretending?

After all, while the Hunger Games have many rules—and part of the deception is the way rules change midway through the fray—there is one rule Katniss believes is immutable: the lone victor takes no prisoners, leaves no survivors. The Games have always worked that way—until now, when the Gamemakers pull a double switch-a-roo. Their first change—two tributes from the same district can both be victors if they are the last two tributes standing. But when Peeta and Katniss emerge victorious, the rules abruptly change back again—only one of them will be permitted to live. It's a deception it does not occur to Katniss to be wary of, and one she refuses to abide by. With bold defiance, she uses her knack for circumventing the Capitol's rules to save both herself and Peeta.

Of course, Katniss' defiance brings severe repercussions. Mid-action Katniss doesn't consider what this will mean for her after the Games, or for her mother and Prim. In retrospect this seems naïve of her—after her time in the arena, hasn't she learned that nothing is certain in the shifting realities of Snow's Panem?

The reward of the Games has always been security and freedom from want for the victor (or in this case, victors) and his or her family. But Katniss' bitter lesson comes via President Snow. He decrees that if she doesn't obey his new directives, everything and everyone she loves will be destroyed. His directives are simple: continue the charade of love for Peeta or else. Later we learn that the idea that winning the Games means safety and happiness is itself a deception, and not just for Katniss. Haymitch should have been a clue, but it is not until Finnick shocks Panem with a tell-all on a rebellion-controlled broadcast that we truly understand how much of a lie it is. "In a flat removed tone . . . " Finnick tells us that his image as "golden boy" back in the Capitol was a sham (*Mockingjay*). The glamor and glitter of his life as a victor cloaks a truly sordid reality: handsome, desirable, idolized by the viewers of the Games, Finnick was condemned by Snow to serve as a sex slave, forced to sell his body to Snow's allies as a favor or to other wealthy Capitol denizens for great sums of money destined for Snow's deep pockets. Refusing to follow Snow's orders was unthinkable. Any protest would doom the people he loved.

Finnick's revelations unmask the real post-Games plight of the victors: there's no safe house to return to from the arena. No promises will be kept. As long as they live they can never drop their guards again.

Who's on My Side, Anyway?

As challenging as discerning the Capitol's deceptions proves, both inside the arena and out, it is the question of whom Katniss can trust that most plagues her. As the series progresses, Katniss grows increasingly aware of hidden agendas: In *The Hunger Games*, Peeta's, Haymitch's, and certainly Snow's; in *Catching Fire*, Plutarch Heavensbee's, Cinna's, and some of the leaders and members of the rebellion's; in *Mockingjay*, of course there is Coin. Who's telling the truth? Who knew what and when? As Katniss puts it very clearly in *Mockingjay* when she critiques her own performance for the propo in support of the rebels, she becomes ". . . a puppet being manipulated by unseen forces." Though referring at that point only to her bad performance in the scripted propo, she might as well be talking about her appropriation by the rebellion.

Trust is a dangerous commodity in Panem. In the first book, even in the relative seclusion of the forest Katniss lowers her voice when discussing the reaping with Gale because "even here you worry someone would hear you." As it turns out, this was not just paranoia—Snow reveals the fact that her hunting excursions with Gale—including the one time they actually kissed—were all reported to him.

Katniss knows she cannot trust the Capitol. But even the behavior of those she should be able to trust is frequently revealed to be questionable—at times even purposely deceitful.

Haymitch: Not What You See, Not What You Get

Haymitch—oh, dear drunken Haymitch. The old souse is a walking—more like a *staggering*—conundrum. Rereading *The Hunger Games* I realize even from the moment where Katniss is standing on stage after the citizens of the district give her their silent farewell salute, he saves her losing her stoic demeanor and bursting into tears. Utterly blotto, he stumbles onto the stage and shouts how he likes her, she's got "spunk," and then he actually points to the Capitol's TV cameras taping the whole event, and seemingly taunts the Capitol by saying she has more spunk "than you!" Then he tumbles off the stage.

Haymitch's continued inebriation is no act, and yet he is startlingly aware—in the way that a long-term alcoholic can be—of exactly what is going on around him and what he is doing. So is his act spontaneous or staged? Is he calculating to get the cameras off Katniss? Is his boozy diatribe a drunken outburst, or is it a message to the Capitol?

From the very first book we know Haymitch is more than what he first appears. He is more than capable of making decisions without consulting those his decisions affect—as when he has Peeta announce his feelings for Katniss during the pregame interview without warning Katniss ahead of time. Yet Katniss trusts him enough to broker a deal in *Catching Fire*: Haymitch and Peeta collaborated to save her in the first Games; in the Quarter Quell, it's Peeta's turn to be saved. But after being rescued from the arena, she is furious to learn that deal was a ruse and the rebellion leaders, with Haymitch's input, opted to save her, not Peeta. On the hovercraft she physically strikes out at him.

During *Mockingjay* she puts as much distance between them as she can in such tight quarters, still stung by his betrayal. Katniss frequently refuses to obey him, ripping off her earpiece when sent into District 8, ignoring his orders, and almost getting herself killed. Her feelings toward Haymitch are complicated: part of her is glad he is undergoing terrible withdrawal symptoms in the teetotalling environment of District 13. But later she worries he is so sick he might die. Then the next moment she reminds herself she doesn't care. When they do finally have face-to-face time alone, they both admit they failed to keep Peeta safe—though nothing they could have done in the arena would have saved him. The guilt they both feel is not resolved, and yet they are at least honest with each other. And by the end of the book she at least trusts that he will understand why she says "yes" to Coin's proposal for one last Hunger Games and that he will back her up by saying yes, too.

Though Haymitch rarely does what Katniss wants him to, he at least does seem to have her long-range interests at heart. The architects behind the rebellion itself, as we and Katniss eventually learn, have little regard for Katniss' best interests at all.

District 13: From Mirage to Fun-House Mirror

I so wanted to root for District 13.

When the mirage is dispelled at the end of *Catching Fire* and we learn that District 13 is a real brick-and-mortar place, I cheered. But this is Panem after all, and what seems to be real never is. For soon the ugly truth is revealed. The district proves to be a distorted mirror-image of the Capitol itself.

District 13's continued existence is more than hinted at in *Catching Fire* during Katniss' encounter in the Forest with District 8 escapees Bonnie and Twill, who clue her in to the looped tape of 13's devastation that the Capitol has been using in its TV broadcasts. Even so, it's a shock to both Katniss and us when 13 has a hovercraft, not to mention a fully functioning underground society. As Katniss learns, 13 is the real "seat" of the rebellion, the brains and part of the brawn behind it all. Thirteen still possesses nuclear weapons, airpower, and a population where everyone is trained to be a soldier.

When the reader first enters District 13 there is no inkling of how it has managed not just to survive the earlier rebellion, but how it continues to exist. How it is able to welcome the refugees from District 12? It integrated them immediately into its community—under the condition that they adhere to the austere conditions: the strict enforcement of food rationing; the requisite military training; the martinet-like adherence to minute-by-minute schedules.

Along with Katniss, we gradually discover that District 13 has not welcomed the survivors out of kindness—oh, no! It has acted primarily to replenish its population, recently decimated by a pox that left many of the survivors infertile—Katniss notices the relative paucity of children in the district.

And then we meet Coin. Alma Coin is the president of the District. Katniss' gut reaction to her—something that, by this point in the series, the reader trusts—is wonderfully described by Collins: "Her eyes are gray . . . The color of slush that you wish would melt away" (*Mockingjay*). There is a cold, calculating quality to Coin—and comparing her eyes to "slush" foreshadows that she is really a counterpoint and twisted mirror image of the Capitol's President Snow.

We learn that District 13's survival occurred because of a kind of "deal with the devil" they negotiated with the Capitol. After all, it was only 13 and the Capitol that possessed nuclear weapons—enough to blow most of Panem to bits and to render the whole country a radioactive wasteland. So the Capitol let 13 survive on the condition that District 13 be portrayed as a smoldering, uninhabited ruin through the fakery of old video tape aired endlessly on TV. Thirteen made the deal, and the appalling images of 13's destruction quenched the burgeoning rebellion. No other district wanted to meet the same fate. On this make-believe foundation the Capitol built its tyrannical reign.

District 13 did not just go away, however. Instead, it bided its time, until it could launch a new rebellion. Its tentacles were carefully spread through many districts, and we learn at the end of *Catching Fire* that at least in terms of saving Katniss in the Quarter Quell, tributes from Districts 3, 4, 7, 8, and 11 were in on the plan.

But as the story plunges into out-and-out guerilla warfare, the mask of Coin's idealism begins to crack. Coin not only plans to have Katniss conveniently killed, a move worthy of Snow, but her plans after the rebels take the Capitol and imprison Snow show that her own innate corruption and evil matches Snow to the letter—not the "final" Games she proposes, but the way she goes about proposing them. By having the surviving victors of the Games vote on whether the children of the Capitol should become arena tributes, she defends herself against any blame. It's a move calculated to keep her above public censure. She could tell the populace that sentencing more children to death was not her decision.

Alma Coin's twisted ambition isn't District 13's only mirror-image of Capitol corruption. Though the seeming reality of District 13's culture is one of great discipline, the militaristic code of the place leads to unspeakable horrors that reflect back the images of torture practiced in the Capitol.

The imprisonment of Katniss' prep team is one example.

After their kidnapping from the Capitol, Flavius, Octavia, and Venia are certainly treated no worse than the refugees from District 12. Their punishment for repeatedly breaking the rules and hoarding an extra piece of bread, we're told, is the same as any native of 13 would have experienced. But the prison conditions would have been torturous for anyone, and are especially so for those unused to any hardship or want. And couching their extended imprisonment as needed discipline is a ruse that fools no one from the Capitol (Fulvia and Plutarch Heavensbee), and certainly not Katniss, Haymitch, or Gale.

If any good comes out of Katniss' discovery of her prep team's plight, it's that she is able to verbalize what she has only suspected up to that point: Coin's corruption. "'Punishing my prep team's a warning,' I tell Fulvia and Heavensbee. 'Not just to me. But to you, too. About who's really in control and what happens if she's not obeyed'" (*Mockingjay*). Coin, and by extension the district, has become a warped mirror-image of the very regime they wish to destroy—and the least trustworthy bunch in the series.[4]

Gale: The Guy She Used to Know

In District 13, during *Mockingjay*, we also see Katniss and Gale move further and further apart. At the end of *Catching Fire*, when Katniss learns that Peeta has not been saved, only Gale can penetrate her pain and despair. At this point it's only Gale who she feels she can still trust.

In *The Hunger Games* Katniss declares, "In the woods waits the only person with whom I can be myself. Gale." An interesting observation: she cannot totally be herself even with her beloved Prim, the little sister for whom she has risked her life. If Prim inadvertently, innocently repeats anything critical of the government, imprisonment, torture, or worse would befall the whole family. As for her mother—Katniss considers her too weak to trust. Certainly she's too unreliable to protect Prim.

Right through the end of *Catching Fire* Katniss continues to trust Gale. He alone has not betrayed or lied to her. His presence on the District 13 rescue helicopter shocks her, but the fact he *is* there at her most desperate hour of need reaffirms their abiding friendship. He has turned up in spite of his having to witness, during the Quarter Quell broadcasts, her declarations of love for Peeta and the "fact" of her pregnancy— knowing only Peeta could be the father. Gale is the rock she

---

4. Snow's agenda is more upfront. As Snow tells Katniss in *Mockingjay*, "I think we'll make this whole situation a lot simpler by agreeing not to lie to each other." And Katniss to her surprise answers, "Yes, I think that would save time."

can lean on and trust, no matter what other fate befalls her. Her faith in Gale crumbles, however, beneath the weight of his betrayal in *Mockingjay*.

Betrayal is close kin to deception, more insidious because only someone you have confided in or bared your heart to, someone you trusted completely, can really betray you. And because of that, the most shattering betrayal Katniss experiences is ultimately by Gale, even though his betrayal is unintentional and not aimed at Katniss. She is just a wounded bystander. Poisoned by the horror of the Capitol's offenses and of war, he becomes so hardened that he is now incapable of understanding how Katniss can't share his "take no survivors" mentality.

When, finally able to go hunting in District 13, they are able to talk in private for the first time since Katniss' rescue, their conversation ultimately leads to a fight. Gale questions her defense of her prep team, recovering at that time under her mother's care in the district's medical center. Katniss tries to explain to him that they are simple in a child-like way—that they really cared for her—and that the penalty for stealing bread is not so very different from Gale's whipping by Thread back home for hunting a turkey. Her arguments fall flat—even for herself. She feels Gale may be right; at the same time her heart tells her he is wrong.

Gale's next betrayal further ruptures Katniss' sense of trust. After Katniss and Finnick accidently witness a devastating broadcast of Peeta's second interview, Katniss waits for Gale to tell her about it. He never does—even though she asks—until eventually she forces him to admit that he knew about it. He lied to her by omission.

By the time Gale and Beetee engineer the collapse of the mountain in District 2, Katniss sees that Gale has become—or perhaps always was—someone whose compassion extends only to a small sphere of family and friends. Anyone, and as it turns out *everyone*—including, depending on how one reads the events at the end of *Mockingjay*, Prim—can be sacrificed to serve the greater good. Ends justify even the most amoral means. It is a true betrayal of all that motivates Katniss' personal and eventually "public" life as the Mockingjay.

Gale's own knife-sharp sense of right and wrong gets increasingly blunted as the tale unfolds, until the one person Katniss trusted in the first book becomes someone whose heart and mind is closed to her by the end of the story.

The Peeta Factor

Whereas Katniss' early relationship with Gale is characterized by trust, her relationship with Peeta, in all three books, is characterized by *mis*trust. She must, from the beginning, see Peeta as an enemy—or at best, a wary, untrustworthy, temporary ally. Only one of them can win the Hunger Games; only one of them can come back alive.

Katniss is accustomed to mistrust, and it is easy to turn it on Peeta. As she witnesses Peeta approaching their train to the Capitol in *The Hunger Games* all puffy-eyed and blotchy from crying, her reaction is swift, her judgment brutal: Is this part of his strategy? To appear weak and soft-hearted? Immediately she questions the reality of Peeta's emotions; and through Katniss' suspicion, Collins plants our own doubts. Is Peeta all about tactics, or is his open, good-hearted nature the real thing? Later on, is his declaration of love for Katniss during Cesar Flickerman's interview for real—or part of some Machiavellian ability to scheme?

Katniss' suspicions, however, are not written in stone—far from it. One minute she is sure Peeta has allied himself with the

Careers to kill her; only a short time later when she is sick and disoriented from tracker jacker venom she realizes "Peeta Mellark just saved my life" (*The Hunger Games*).

Before entering the arena for the first time, during the interview with Cesar Flickerman, Peeta catches her totally off guard when he declares shyly that the one girl he's ever had a crush on is Katniss, the fellow tribute he will be compelled to kill if he wants to be the victor.

Not only is she shocked, she's furious. She actually shoves him when they are alone. But her anger and confusion mount exponentially when she learns that Haymitch and Peeta had discussed this whole approach before the interview: Peeta in love with Katniss. A brilliant strategy. But the idea that Peeta is telling the truth still haunts her. Does he actually care for her?

As Haymitch reminds her in that same scene when she insists they are not star-crossed lovers, "Who cares? It's all a big show. It's how you're perceived" (*The Hunger Games*).

When it comes to something as personal as romance, Katniss instinctively recoils. Although she is sixteen at the start of the trilogy, she has never given any conscious thought to romance.[5] And then there is Gale back home, rooting for her and at the same time witness to Peeta's televised declaration. Katniss can't help but wonder about the effect on him, which makes her begin to wonder about her own feelings—and yet, as Haymitch says, it's all just an act, and one that serves her well.

However, this act becomes even more difficult to pull off in *Catching Fire*. After Snow dictates the course of her future with

5. Rather, her one thought is she never wants to marry and have children. All children born in Panem are destined to become future tributes in the Hunger Games—a fate Katniss refuses to accept for anyone she loves ever again, if she can help it.

Peeta, Peeta himself throws another wrench into the works. He announces she is pregnant. Katniss is horrified, and yet has to play along—and then realizes of course that this gives her another advantage both in the arena and with sponsors. While Katniss is expert at negotiating deceptions to achieve her aims, Peeta, like Haymitch, is expert at achieving his aims by creating them.[6]

To further complicate matters, Katniss is not sure of her own feelings. Is she falling in love? By the end of *Catching Fire*, neither we nor she is sure. But Katniss has finally come to a place where she trusts his feelings if nothing else. Which is, naturally, when she learns she cannot—when a rescued Peeta turns out to have been hijacked and does not love her at all anymore, his memories manipulated into cruel versions of reality in which Katniss is his enemy.

The whole series, and Peeta and Katniss' entire relationship, is fraught with the challenge of distinguishing reality from unreality, but Peeta's hijacking may best illustrate the overriding conundrum of the series. Not only can Katniss not trust Peeta, but Peeta cannot even trust himself.

In District 13 they remain largely separated as Peeta is treated, but when the rebels invade the Capitol, Coin sends Peeta into battle alongside Katniss. His better self has been partially reclaimed, but he is still unable to tell real memories from altered ones and is still unstable, with unpredictable violent outbursts—all aimed at Katniss.

Though he is heavily guarded, Katniss remains wary. One minute his behavior is normal; the next minute it is lethal. Katniss' own feelings swing wildly: Can she trust him or not? Peeta's

---

6. His fiction about Katniss' pregnancy is in a way an extension of his talent at camouflage, an ability Katniss makes fun of when they are in the Training Center but one that saves his life in the arena when, injured, he hides in plain sight, using mud and leaves to blend in to the ground. He is so good that even Katniss does not see him until she almost steps on him.

untrustworthiness is Snow's fault, not his own, but that doesn't change the reality that if Katniss guesses wrong at any moment and lets down her guard, she could die.

Her eventual reclamation of their friendship begins with a game of "Real or Not Real"—a poignantly explicit version of the game the two of them have been playing all along. Through it, they are able to find their way back to each other, until, just prior to the epilogue, when Peeta asks: "'You love me. Real or not real?'" Katniss is at last able to tell him, "'Real'" (*Mockingjay*).

Katniss: Know Yourself, Be Yourself

The reason this exchange is so important is that, of all the people Katniss feels she cannot trust, at various times and in various ways, during the course of the series, the most important is herself.

Smoke and fog—literal and figurative—engulf Katniss throughout the Hunger Games. Toxic fogs in the arena and oily miasmas that fill the alleys and streets of the Capitol battleground threaten her very survival. But the hardest to penetrate is her own blindness: she cannot read the state of her heart. What does she feel? And for whom?

One or two feelings are perfectly clear to her:[7] Her unequivocal

---

7. Oh, yes, Katniss' feelings are unequivocal when it comes to one other creature. She really hates Buttercup. She wishes often she'd drowned him instead of giving him to Prim. But eventually she embraces him as a remnant of all she has ever loved in Prim, the way, when someone close to you dies, even the scent lingering on a shirt, or dress, brings you momentarily close to that person's spirit. Buttercup holds a bit of Prim inside of him and by the end of Katniss' journey she also finds him one of her most trusted companions. His loyalty and fierceness, after all, matches her own.

love for Prim. Her hatred of President Snow. Perhaps one can also add in a more general way her deep sense of the immorality and horror of the Games.

What makes Katniss a compelling heroine is that she is a bundle of contradictions. She's a pro at hiding her feelings beneath a stony, angry exterior; at the same time she's a terrible actress. Whenever she has to "perform"—to *sell* herself—to an audience, she's a flop. It's Cinna who tells her from the outset to "be herself," to "be honest"—Cinna's job is to create artifice, and yet confronted with Katniss, he sees that she shines best in her own light, with her own natural beauty and manner. And this is a clue to the "real" Katniss, the person she herself is not yet acquainted with.

Katniss frequently doubts her own motivations. For a time she even becomes caught up in Peeta's post-hijacking delusions. Her own guilt about the devastation her actions seem to have triggered—the destruction of District 12, so many people's pain, suffering, and death—mounts. Is she really a cold-blooded killer? She slaughters other tributes in the arenas; she longs to murder Snow. What kind of person does that make her? One incapable of feeling? She fears all this, and Peeta's Capitol-induced rants home in on her own sense of failure and guilt and seem to confirm her suspicions: "Finally he sees me for who I really am. Violent. Distrustful. Manipulative. Deadly" (*Mockingjay*). She grows increasingly confused. If Peeta, the one person who has always thought the best of her, can be convinced of all this, what must others think of her? What should she think of herself?

A lovely summation of just what other people think about Katniss appears in *Mockingjay* right after she has failed miserably while rehearsing a scripted propo. Much to her chagrin,

Haymitch takes control of the situation and asks the group gathered in Command exactly when Katniss during the Games made them *"feel* something real" (*Mockingjay*). The answers come, and with every memory we, if not yet Katniss, are assured she is neither a cold-hearted killer nor incapable of love. It's her acting that is pathetic, not the state of her heart.

Because Katniss has been so hurt in the past, she has built a barrier around her heart. Or maybe, in the language of these Games, she has become ensnared by pain. She is defensive. She cannot believe people would love her—until in desperate circumstances she has no choice but to see that they do. Not just her closest acquaintances and friends, but strangers, like the injured in the hospital in District 8 who, even maimed or dying, recognize her face and reach for her, joyful that she is alive to carry on the cause—everyone who has been inspired by her fiery determination to right horrendous wrongs.

Ultimately Katniss is able to admit that at times she has acted from the part of her that is Snow's—and perhaps Coin's— equal. Her unerring instinct for survival has made her behave in ways her better self isn't proud of. But ultimately, too, she is able to make peace with her role. By seeing and embracing who she truly is, good and bad, she is able to see through one of the Capitol's greatest illusions: that she is responsible for the rebellion, rather than merely the means by which they were overthrown.

Katniss discovers that, even after all she has been through and all she has lost, she is still capable of love. That Snow and the evils of the Capitol have not stolen the possibility of new beginnings, or of having children, for whom the Games will be old history. In the end, the smoke clears and the mirror reflects only the truth—only what is real.

ELIZABETH M. REES *is a writer and visual artist living in Greenwich Village in New York City. She has published numerous young adult books, including* The Wedding, *a novel set in fifteenth century Bruges featuring the painter Jan Van Eyck. She is currently working on a series of short stories about the afterlife and is continuing to weave a tale of an often elusive fat fairy named Maeve.*

SOMEONE TO WATCH OVER ME

▶

Power and Surveillance in the Hunger Games

LILI WILKINSON

The power in Panem all seems to lie with the Capitol—or more precisely, with President Snow and his government. In the Hunger Games, the same is true of the Gamemakers. After all, they engineer the action: they decide not only what will happen to the tributes, but also what the people at home will see. As the events of the Hunger Games series show, however, the idea that the engineers are all-powerful is an illusion. Those watching at home, and those (like Katniss) being watched, have power too. Lili Wilkinson looks at the delicate balance between these three groups and at how even a small shift in power can mean change on a massive scale.

It must be very fragile, if a handful of berries can bring it down.
—Katniss Everdeen, *Catching Fire*

A few hundred years ago, if you did something wrong you were physically punished—beaten or even hanged, usually in front of a crowd. The whole point of this was to warn the people watching—if you do something bad, this could happen to you. Except it didn't quite work. Because if you're watching a starving thirteen-year-old girl being flogged for stealing a loaf of bread, you're not thinking about what a terrible person she is, and how you'd better not ever do anything like that. You're thinking, *That poor girl. She only wanted something to eat.* And the people who are doing the punishing don't want you to feel sorry for her.

So in the nineteenth century things changed. Instead of physically hurting criminals, we started to put them in prison. And the thing about prison is, you're always being watched, by guards and (nowadays) security cameras. Even if there isn't actually anyone watching you at that second, there *might* be, and you've got no way of knowing. Sound familiar? It should, because this doesn't just happen in prisons. It also happens in schools, hospitals, factories—even walking down the street, chances are you're being watched by a surveillance camera.

Are you starting to feel a bit creeped out?

Surveillance is at the heart of the Hunger Games, and the Hunger Games trilogy. But in addition to using surveillance for the sake of safety and control, the Games are surveillance for the sake of *entertainment*. The watchers aren't guards or lawmakers, they're just everyday viewers, at home in their living rooms. And there is a third group, as well—the Gamemakers, the people behind the camera, the people who engineer and shape what the viewers see. Each of these groups—the Watched, the Watchers, and the Engineers—has a little power of its own. But what happens when one group has too much control?

The Watched

Next time you leave the house, think about who might be watching you. Do you pass a traffic camera? Do the shops you go to have security cameras? Is there a camera on board your train or bus? What about in your school? The cafes and restaurants where you eat? Street corners? Subways? And who is on the other side of that camera? A private security guard? The police? The government? How can you tell?

Surveillance changes the way we behave. When you eat a meal in a busy restaurant, why don't you just walk out without paying? It's likely nobody would even notice, let alone try and stop you. So why don't you do it? Well, firstly, you wouldn't because you know that it would be unfair to the chef who cooked your meal, and the waiters who served you. But *really* the reason is because you're afraid someone's watching, and you might get caught. And it's this fear that explains the existence of security cameras.

There are over a million security cameras in London, which is more than one camera for every seven people living there. In 2008, a Metropolitan Police report found that only one crime was solved per thousand cameras, and surveillance has uncovered no acts of terrorism. Security cameras don't *solve* crime—instead they are there as a warning, to try and stop people from committing crimes in the first place, because *you never know who might be watching*. Similarly, not letting you take your water bottle on a plane isn't a measure to catch terrorists—it's to make you (and hopefully potential wrongdoers) afraid. Someone *might* be watching you, so you'd better behave, or else there'll be consequences.

This idea that you're always being watched is what makes the Hunger Games so powerful. Katniss and the other tributes know that at any time they could be on television, their deeds and actions being transmitted across Panem, into the homes of strangers, friends, family, and, most importantly, the people who run the Games. So Katniss knows that every single thing she does will affect people everywhere—it might result in Gale's heart being broken, or cause her family shame, or worse, her loved ones may be tortured or killed.

The watching is completely one-way in *The Hunger Games*. On her first night in the arena, Katniss looks up to the sky and sees the faces of each dead tribute, but there is no live footage:

> At home, we would be watching full coverage of each and every killing, but that's thought to give an unfair advantage to the living tributes. For instance, if I got my hands on the bow and shot someone, my secret would be revealed to all. (*The Hunger Games*)

She is being observed by every citizen in Panem, but she can't look back into their living rooms and see who's watching. She can't even see what the other tributes are doing. Although everyone can see her, Katniss is completely alone. But she knows she's being watched, and who the Watchers are. And she knows how to influence them.

The tributes are always aware of the cameras, even if they can't see them. After Katniss overhears Peeta with the career

tributes on the first night of the Games, she understands that
she can create drama by revealing her presence to the cameras.
She knows she's guaranteed a close-up:

> Until I work out exactly how I want to play that, I'd better
> at least act on top of things. Not perplexed. Certainly not
> confused or frightened. No, I need to look one step ahead of
> the game. (*The Hunger Games*)

Katniss plays up to the camera, stepping into the light,
pausing, cocking her head and giving a knowing smile. She
realizes displaying her hunting skills will make her attractive to
sponsors. And when she starts to weaken, an injured leg possibly
spelling her doom, Katniss is sure the cameras are on her face,
meaning that she can't show her pain or fear: "Pity does not get
you aid. Admiration at your refusal to give in does" (*The Hunger
Games*). At first, Katniss is just trying to play the game—to
appeal to sponsors who can help her survive. But then things
start to change. Katniss starts to use her position, her visibility,
as a message. She decorates Rue's body with flowers as a protest
against the unrelenting violence of the Games.

Then come the berries. Katniss realizes that she has the power
to save both herself and Peeta. She threatens the Capitol and the
Gamemakers with an Engineer's disaster—a reality TV show
with no ending. No winner. No Victory Tour. No interviews.
The ultimate letdown. And so the Gamemakers relent, and let
them both live.

Katniss' power—the power of the Watched—lies in her
ability to influence the Watchers. She can give them what they
want—heroic deeds, drama, romance. And once she is a favorite
of the Watchers, she has a kind of safety from the ruthless
Engineers. Because the Engineers know that if the viewers are

left unhappy—if there is an unsatisfying ending to the Hunger Games—the whispers of rebellion among the Watchers might grow to shouts.

The Watchers

The Hunger Games trilogy was inspired by the Ancient Greek story of Theseus and the Minotaur. In Theseus' story, selected tributes are sent from Athens to a labyrinth, where a hungry monster waits to devour them. The families and friends of the tributes must say farewell to them when they leave—knowing they'll never see their loved ones again.

The Hunger Games is different. In the Hunger Games, the hungry beast isn't a real monster; instead it's the Watchers—the thousands of citizens watching at home. In the Hunger Games, the families and friends *will* see their loved ones again—on television, every night, at prime time.

The Athenian people in the Greek myth were terrified of their children being sent to their deaths, but although the Districts dread the reaping, all of Panem tunes in to watch the Hunger Games as eagerly as we tune in to watch *Survivor* or *American Idol*. Why do they watch it? Do they really enjoy seeing their children murder each other? Why don't they refuse to watch? What would happen if every citizen in Panem just turned off the television?

But nobody does. The viewers at home are just as bloodthirsty and eager for drama as we are when watching an episode of *The Bachelorette* or *The Amazing Race*. What does that say about the people of Panem? What does it say about the way they and their society are controlled? And what does it say about us?

Some of our most popular TV shows are a bit like the Hunger

Games. Sure, nobody dies on our reality TV shows. But we still watch people suffer. We watch them endure physical and mental challenges on *Survivor*, subject them to isolation on *Big Brother*, tell them their dreams will never come true on *Idol*, and break their hearts on *The Bachelorette*. Reality TV is all about putting people in difficult situations and watching how they react. Some people come out stronger, richer, and healthier, facing a lifetime of success. Others are voted off the island early on, their failure broadcast all over the world. How many steps are there, between our own TV shows and the Hunger Games?

What about *Temptation Island*, a TV show that tries to pressure couples into cheating on one another? Or *Shattered*, a UK show where contestants must go without sleep for seven days? Or *Extreme Makeover*, where people are permanently, surgically altered to conform to some kind of Hollywood ideal of beauty? And what about the violence of *Ultimate Fighter*, *Celebrity Boxing*, and *Bad Girls Club*? Suddenly the Hunger Games isn't looking quite as science fiction as it was before, is it?

Just like real-life TV producers, the Gamemakers must keep the Watchers entertained. And the Watchers are so entranced by Katniss' story—so won over by her fierce bravery and kind heart—that if she vanishes from their screens, they might do the unthinkable. They might switch off.

The Watchers of Panem respond strongly to the star-crossed romance of Peeta and Katniss. They latch on to it and show their support. And what happens? *The rules of the game change.* The Gamemakers milk the romance and the drama for all it's worth—the viewers get to see Katniss nurse Peeta back to health. In everyone's eyes, the two are desperately in love and wholly focused on surviving and protecting each other. But then the rules change again, and the balance of power swings back to the Engineers. Suddenly Peeta and Katniss are enemies once more, the Capitol determined to create the most dramatic season finale ever. But it backfires. Katniss holds up those blue berries, and changes the rules herself. It's one thing to present the drama-hungry Watchers with the tragic death of one of the lovers, but it's another thing altogether to have *two* deaths. Two deaths would mean no victor. No Victory Tour. The Engineers are forced to back down, and allow Katniss and Peeta to claim their shared victory.

The Engineers

The thing about Panem is that for the most part, its citizens don't know they're being oppressed. They think the Capitol is there to look out for them, to protect them. They are told that having their children taken away each year and slaughtered on television is a warning, wrapped up in an easily digestible prime-time viewing experience. And because each district is closed off, surrounded by barbed wire and guard towers, nobody really knows what's going on. Nobody sees the starvation and poverty in District 12, or the decadence and waste in the Capitol.

Except Katniss. She realizes the truth when she goes on her Victory Tour and sees how bad it is in the districts. But can she do anything about it? No. Because she can't escape the cameras. Even outside the arena, Katniss is still being filmed, everywhere she goes. The Hunger Games may have finished, but the Katniss Everdeen Show is still going. The Engineers are still using her to control the Watched. President Snow is unhappy with the swing of power toward the Watched and the Watchers, so he threatens Katniss and her family. He tells her that she must convince the citizens of Panem that the stunt with the berries was an act of love, not an act of defiance or rebellion. Snow knows that just as Katniss can be the spark that could destroy Panem, she can also be used to calm the Watchers down—to be a loyal and obedient citizen. To swing the balance of power back to the Engineers.

It doesn't take Katniss long to realize that her return to District 12 after the first Hunger Games isn't a return to anonymity. She's still one of the Watched:

> Surely they haven't been tracking us in there. Or have they? Could we have been followed? That seems impossible. At least by a person. Cameras? That never crossed my mind until this moment. (*Catching Fire*)

In *Mockingjay*, the whole of Panem is turned into a kind of giant arena—broadcast every night in full color, complete with titles and a stirring soundtrack. The war seems to be less about fighting over physical territory, and more about fighting over control of the airwaves—whose propo (short for propaganda) will dominate? Who can spin the war to the best advantage?

When Katniss watches the propo from District 8, she doesn't try to imagine herself back in the thick of combat. She tries to pretend she's watching her television back in District 12. Instead of thinking that something was happening *in Panem* that has never happened before, she thinks that there's "never been anything like it *on television*." It's like the whole war is an elaborate promotional tool for the rebellion to broadcast its agenda. Katniss joins a specially trained elite squad of soldiers—soldiers not trained in combat skills, but in media skills—to be the "on-screen faces of the invasion." They're followed by a camera team wherever they go, and all of the death, destruction, violence, and suffering is neatly packaged up every night and delivered to living rooms everywhere. Suddenly the people behind the cameras have *all* the power, and both Watcher and Watched become tools to promote and spread propaganda.

In *Catching Fire*, President Snow uses Katniss' family and loved ones as a bargaining chip—if she behaves and puts on a good show, they get to live. Katniss realizes quickly that she can't run away from the cameras or the crowds—they'll always find her. And even when she does escape the power of Snow and joins the rebellion in *Mockingjay*, she finds herself doing exactly the same thing. She's still got her prep team, she's still surrounded by cameras insisting she put on a good show, and she's still working for someone who has the power to destroy her loved ones. A group of Watchers—the people of Panem who so passively consumed the Games in the past—have taken control of cameras and screens. The rebel Watchers are now Engineers.

The Balancing Act

In *Mockingjay*, the delicate balance of power swings toward the Engineers, and Katniss becomes a pawn in a new game, a dangerous struggle between the Capitol Engineers and the rebel Engineers.

> The full impact of what I've done hits me. It was not intentional—I only meant to express my thanks—but I have elicited something dangerous. An act of dissent from the people of District Eleven. This is exactly the kind of thing I am supposed to be defusing! (*Catching Fire*)

When Katniss is captured by the rebels and pressured to become the face of the rebellion, she thinks she understands the power that she holds as the Mockingjay:

> A new sensation begins to germinate inside me . . . Power. I have a kind of power I never knew I possessed. (*Mockingjay*)

But Katniss' power is slipping away, slowly being eradicated by the rebel Watchers-turned-Engineers from the moment she is rescued from her second Hunger Games. In District 2, Haymitch dictates Katniss' speech to her through her headset. Her prep team control the way she looks and what she wears. Her actions and words are carefully edited into bite-sized, easily digestible pieces of propaganda. Her participation in the rebellion is just as choreographed and controlled as her participation in the Hunger Games. In fact, Katniss had *more* power and control *within* the Games—playing up to the cameras, winning over the Watchers, threatening to eat the berries and shooting down the forcefield—than she does when she's part of the rebellion. The only time she comes close to this kind of independence and agency outside the arena is in *Mockingjay* when she's declared dead—because the cameras can't see her any more (and aren't looking for her), she can finally make her own decisions.

Through her trials in the Arena and her participation in the war, Katniss comes to learn that surveillance isn't a one-way street. When she threatens to eat the blue berries, she forces the Capitol to change the rules of the Games. This saves her life and Peeta's, but it marks her as a Rebel, and an enemy of the Capitol. The balance of power swings her way—for a moment. But in *Catching Fire*, President Snow takes it back. He amps up his surveillance, watching Katniss wherever she goes, ready to pounce if she steps out of line. Rebellion is brewing, and to threaten and control Katniss even further, he sends her back into the Games. But that turns out to be his greatest mistake. Like that poor girl who stole a loaf of bread, the Watchers at home don't feel threatened, or bloodthirsty. They love Katniss, and they are sick of the Engineers taking away their riches and their children. Katniss very quickly realizes that for every act of cruelty and terror that the Capitol punishes her with in the Games, she is provided with an opportunity. To spread dissent and rebellion throughout Panem, and to unify the Watchers and the Watched into an unstoppable force.

When Katniss wins over the hearts of the Watchers and earns the hatred of the Engineers, she becomes a spark, a spark which, in the words of President Snow, grows to "an inferno that destroys Panem." But starting a fire doesn't mean you can control it. Katniss starts the rebellion, but events quickly move beyond her control. Her power is fleeting, and largely symbolic. Before long, the rebel Engineers take over, and the old balance between Watcher, Watched, and Engineer is restored.

Mockingjay finishes with Katniss living in uneasy, troubled peace. She's no longer Watched, but she isn't a Watcher or an Engineer either. She's retired. Plutarch understands Katniss' anxiety—he knows that it's only a matter of time before things disintegrate once more. But he's ready, ever the Engineer, to point his cameras and repackage real-world drama and suffering into popular entertainment. He allows himself a cheerful moment of optimism: "Maybe we are witnessing the evolution of the human race." And then he tells Katniss all about the new *Idol*-style program he's about to launch. Evolution indeed.

Katniss turned around and looked back into the camera that was always watching her—and she changed the world. But she is uneasy because she knows that this new balance between the Watchers, the Watched, and the Engineers won't last forever. Sooner or later, the balance will swing too far in one direction, and the Games will begin all over again.

LILI WILKINSON *is the award-winning author of* Scatterheart *and* Angel Fish. *She lives in Australia where she can usually be found reading, writing, sewing, or consuming quality TV (along with quality chocolate). Her latest book,* Pink, *will be published by HarperCollins in February 2011.*

REALITY HUNGER

▶

Authenticity, Heroism, and Media in the Hunger Games

NED VIZZINI

If there's one quality people look for in their reality television show contestants, it's their ability to be "real"—to appear genuine, in spite of the cameras that follow them around. Should be easy, right? All you have to do is, as Cinna tells Katniss in *The Hunger Games*, "be yourself." But being real is harder than it looks. It's not Katniss herself that the viewers fall for, after all. It's Katniss the star-crossed lover, Katniss the girl on fire, Katniss the Mockingjay. Being real is as much about artifice as it is about reality. Ned Vizzini looks at media training, the challenge of authenticity, and what it really takes to become a media hero, both in Katniss' world and in ours.

When I was nineteen, slightly older than Katniss Everdeen in *The Hunger Games* (and worse at archery), I was invited to leave my home and journey to a faraway land to prepare for a new chapter in my life. The faraway land was not the Capitol but Minneapolis, Minnesota. The new chapter was not a pubescent deathmatch—I had just been through that in high school—but a professional arena where every day contestants young and old are ground up and forgotten, driven to alcoholism, and sent back to graduate school. I was going to be a published author. My publisher had decided that I needed "media training."

I arrived at MSP Airport with scant television experience. In grade school I had been on a Nickelodeon "Big Help" public service ad raking leaves and was given 0.2 seconds of screen time; as an infant I had failed out of auditions for a diaper commercial. (I could still end up in an adult diaper commercial.) The publisher was betting that this track record would change, because I was young enough and likable enough to do talk shows. I had to be ready. Being on television talk shows is a coup for any author. Most of the time if you see an author on TV, you are watching BookTV on CSPAN, and the only other person watching is my father.

An editor met me at the airport. She brought me to a restaurant where I saw "Beer Cheese Soup" on the menu. I learned it was a Minnesota specialty and ordered it. Like the lamb stew that Katniss gushes over in *The Hunger Games,* it blew my mind; I still cannot find anything like it. The editor told me how excited everyone was for my book to be published and how much fun this was going to be. I knew from past experience that this meant *run*.

In **The Hunger Games**, Katniss Everdeen is suspicious of her media training. When she arrives in the Capitol, she notes the strange accents and adornments of her prep team (no comment here on the Minnesota accent, which I found delightful). Not only do members of her team have tinted skin and high-pitched voices, they have a job that is alien to Katniss: to make her look good on television. This expertise in abstraction runs counter to her experience as a hunter and provider in District 12. A world like the Capitol, where food can appear at the touch of a button and image is everything, does not seem real to Katniss, and *realness*—real emotion, real resolve, real fire—is at the heart of *The Hunger Games*.

Katniss becomes famous because of her realness. When Caesar Flickerman asks her in her first televised interview what has impressed her most about the Capitol and she mentions the lamb stew, the laugh she elicits cements a love affair with her public that she contends with for the rest of the trilogy. Why is this answer so important? It is *honest*. It shows a lack of concern for what the "right" answer might be ("the architecture," "the fashion") and, in a world of tightly controlled propaganda, this is revolutionary. It is the first signal to the people of Panem that Katniss is an uncorrupted firebrand—one who has conveniently been on actual fire—and implies that she has no hidden motivations or agendas, unlike the rest of the contestants on the reality program they love so much.

Of course, in order to win the Hunger Games and lead the rebellion that follows, Katniss must betray that realness and employ all sorts of calculated gambits, losing herself in a maze of self-constructed imagery. Once she becomes famous, she is forced to consider how much of her persona is real and how much is fashioned by her many handlers, from Cinna to Haymitch to President Coin—all of whom do not end up well. Thus the Hunger Games presents us with the kind of hero that not only Panem but America likes best: the reluctant one, unexpectedly brilliant when challenged and then, once famous, desirous of a simpler life.

In preparing *The Terminator*, James Cameron studied the narrative characteristics of the ten most successful films of all time. He found a common thread: ordinary people in extraordinary situations.[1] Implicit in "ordinariness" is realness, authenticity, and humility, traits that Katniss has in spades. No wonder the Hunger Games seemed like a good fit for the big screen.

I went to a television studio to meet my media trainer. I will call her Jessica, which might have also been her real name.

Jessica wore a perfectly tailored dark suit. She shook my hand (down-up-down, crisp) while I stared at the ceiling, which was so high that it allowed for wind currents. Humongous lights—like chrome bombs—beamed down on a wide blank area with two chairs.

"That's where we're going to do the practice interview," Jessica said. "But first, makeup!"

I was taken to a back room and plunked in a dental chair. A

---

1. Dana Goodyear, "Man of Extremes: The Return of James Cameron," in *The New Yorker*: http://www.newyorker.com/reporting/2009/10/26/091026fa_fact_goodyear.

alism began to feel like a barrier to entry. *Authenticity*—the ability of a hero to convince an audience that *you could be me*—became paramount, and ordinary people in extraordinary situations became the go-to guys and gals for heroic tales.

In America, this went over particularly well, as it reflected the idea of the American Dream. If an ordinary person can thrive in tremendous peril, an ordinary reader can surely achieve greatness through life's ups and downs. While the Hunger Games sets itself firmly in this tradition, it also addresses a more up-to-date variant of the American Dream: the dream to be famous for no reason at all.

Ask a few kids from Alabama to Wyoming what they want to be when they grow up, and these days you are likely to hear "famous." Not famous for any particular thing, just "famous." It seems unsavory to older ears, but this is a dream rooted in the original American Dream, the one about working hard and getting ahead. The only difference is that technology has removed the need for work.

By the 1920s, the red eye of the motion picture camera could do for human beings what the printing press did for words—make them reproducible at low cost for mass consumption. For the first time, it was possible to be famous for no reason other than an ability to be interesting in front of a camera, because there was such a thing as a camera, and it is a testament to the American work ethic that everyone did not immediately drop what they were doing to ambush one.

Some did, of course. Hopefuls streamed to Hollywood to get into the movie business. Viewers dreamed of television stardom and read magazines about it to be closer to their dream. But work still had a place in media success; the act of *performance* was

still a craft. You did not get to be a star just by being yourself—
you got to be a star by being amazing. "To grasp the full signifi-
cance of life is the actor's duty," said James Dean,[2] which sounds
like the same sort of duty a writer or musician should aspire to.

Then *The Real World* came along. Starting in 1992 and currently picked up by MTV for its twenty-sixth season, the show
was so simple and instantly ubiquitous that it can be hard to
step back and recognize its impact. It took Andy Warhol's 1968
dictum about fifteen minutes of fame and put it to the test every
week. *The Real World* stripped away any value for accomplish-
ment; no one on the show was cool because they had a good job
or created good art (remember the season where they were all
supposed to get jobs?—a disaster!); they were cool because they
were real, and the rise of *The Real World* dovetailed with the
fetishization of the word "real" in hip-hop. Cultural currency no
longer came from acts, it came from realness, as defined by an
ability to be interesting in front of observers while not appearing
to attempt to be interesting. *The Real World* was Zen: the only
thing you had to do to get on it was be real, but if you tried to
be real you would never make it.

By this time too the words "success" and "fame" had been
conflated in American discourse. Kids who watched *The Real
World* did not want to be successful; they wanted to be famous.
They did not understand or care that there was a difference
between the two. The tragic actors and actresses who achieved
fame only to drown in it, from Marilyn Monroe to River Phoenix,
were still famous. The housemates on *The Real World* were famous
for being real and successful for being famous, and for almost a
decade this was enough for the American public. Then *Survivor*

---

2. "James Dean Quotes," ThinkQuest: http://thinkexist.com/quotation/to_
grasp_the_full_significance_of_life_is_the/256995.html.

came along, the brainchild of a British television producer, and reintroduced the Puritan work ethic to the reality media landscape. To be on *Survivor,* all you had to do was be real, but once you were on it, you had to be exceptional again—to compete in challenging competitions and outsmart your opponents. It was a microcosm of the old American Dream inside the new, and like *The Real World* it spawned a host of imitators.

American Idol swung the pendulum back toward the old dream, unfolding season after season like a hyper-speed trip through Hollywood past, with clean, glitzy stages and an unfailing obedience to the will of the people. It rewarded performance in the most traditional way: a straight vote. Critics called *Idol* many things, but they never called it fake.

While it ascended, the *Real World* model of fame for free was picked up by the internet. By 2006, when *Time* magazine's Person of the Year was "You," it was unnecessary—hokey—to appear on television to gain fame. The problem was that on the internet, being real was no longer enough; with 900,000 new blogs created per day,[3] dreamers had to dream bigger to get their message across. The absurd rose to the top—obese singers, dramatic chipmunks, focused light saber artistes. Being real was requisite, but now a certain amount of perversion and disregard for shame was also necessary.

Katniss Everdeen, then, is a post-American dreamer whose story pulls from each stage of the past hundred years of media history. Like the housemates on *The Real World*, she is not selected for the Hunger Games for any particular skill. Her family is struck by the hand of fate in the reaping and she does the best she can in response, selflessly taking the place of her

---

3. Ba Kiwanuka, "900,000 New Blogs Created Everyday Means Yours is Irrelevant Unless . . .": http://www.articlealley.com/article_ 878118_64.html.

younger sister, which is what we would like to think we would do. As an ordinary girl in extraordinary circumstances, her reluctance makes her authentic.

Contrast this with the Careers that she fights against from District 2. Not only are they cunning and bloodthirsty, they *want to be there.* They train for the Hunger Games and look forward to achieving fame and glory on television. They are like the posers who do not make *The Real World*, the boys and girls who try too hard; they are also like Gilgamesh, brutally exceptional in the most unrelatable way. By being willing participants in the Games, they "swallowed the Capitol's propaganda more easily than the rest of us," says Katniss in *Mockingjay*, which makes them dupes, quaintly hokey, buying into a system that does not work. They are holdovers from a generation that believes in work rather than realness as the path to success, while Katniss learns it is authenticity that makes her a heroine in a media-saturated age.

But Katniss' realness is only the beginning. Once her interview brings her to Panem's attention, she delivers in combat, beating the Careers at their own game. Inside the arena, she takes on the traits that made Richard Hatch a hero on *Survivor*—ruthlessness—and Kelly Clarkson a heroine on *American Idol*—skill. The fact that she is drafted into a reality show she then excels at, despite not wanting to, lets her succeed in the old American dream while embracing the new. She is famous for being good and famous for being herself.

I was not good. After my initial choke-up on camera, Jessica asked what the problem was.

"I just sort of . . . started thinking about who might be watching."

"But no one's watching."

"Hypothetically."

"The way to approach a television interview isn't to think about the people watching, Ned, but about the interviewer." Jessica explained further: most people who watch television watch it alone, so if I acted the way I did when I was communicating with a friend, I would appear natural on the other side of the screen. Cinna tells Katniss the same thing to prepare her for her interview with Caesar: "'Suppose, when you answer the questions, you think you're addressing a friend back home'" (*The Hunger Games*).

"I don't know if I'm really that natural when I communicate with my friends."

"Do you look them in the eye?"

"No."

"You should. And you should look your interviewer in the eye."

"Shouldn't I look at the camera?"

She smiled. "You should look at the camera but *not* look at the camera." More Zen. It turns out that the proper way to treat a camera in an interview is to eye it at a three-fourths angle, as if you happen to be *sort of* looking at it while your main focus stays on the interviewer. Like being on *Survivor*, or in the Hunger Games, you need to be real in order for the audience to connect with you. Then you need to play the game in order to win.

Katniss gets put through the gamut during her media training. Prior to her interview, Haymitch attempts to have her act humble, cocky, witty, sexy, and mysterious, to both of their frustration. "'[P]retend I'm the audience,'" he advises. "'Delight me'" (*The Hunger Games*). Katniss does not, and soon enough Haymitch is throwing up his hands, drunk. As a veteran of the Hunger Games he should know better.

"Being aware of the audience leads to overeagerness," Jessica explained, "which television cameras register as *fakeness.*"

"Is that why so many people seem fake on TV?"

"Sometimes. Sometimes they really are fake. Want to try again?"

I nodded. Jessica was my Cinna. Luckily for Katniss, it is Cinna, the unexpected voice of reason, who gets the final word before her interview. He contradicts Haymitch's advice and asks her the question that spurs her to greatness: "'Why don't you just be yourself?'" (*The Hunger Games*).

After her triumph in the Hunger Games, Katniss finds it difficult to stay herself. Her heroism, which begins in authenticity and solidifies in skill, comes under fire as soon as she slips into a public persona, first as victor of the Games and then as the Mockingjay, face of the rebellion. Readers can likely relate to Katniss' struggles to reconcile her personal and private lives, as they also have public profiles to maintain.

It started with blogs; now, through social media, anyone who is active on the internet creates a digital projection of themselves for public consumption. We are all stars, all heroes in our own online productions. What does this do for our authenticity? It destroys it.

The problem is that anyone who checks into Facebook, Twitter, and the like is automatically shown how their profile is trending through wall posts, messages, and friend requests. Anyone who Googles him or herself engages in a form of self-regard that used to require highly paid analysts. A truly authentic hero would not care what others thought; he or she would be comfortable enough to ignore the chatter of digital friends and strangers in lieu of the strength of his or her convictions. But a person who uses social media *does* care what others think—demonstrably. Looking at ourselves on the internet, we are not ourselves, and no amount of rationalization makes us seem like anything other than egotists.

Katniss avoids this pitfall in the Hunger Games through the circumstances of the competition. Thrown into an arena without media access, she cannot tell how she is doing. (Luckily she is not as addicted to social media as the rest of us; for many Hunger Games readers, the lack of an internet connection might be the most difficult part of the Games.) She knows that she is on television but cannot watch it; she must rely on her hunches, which are unquestionably hers, to survive. She is not only genuine, not only skilled; she is incapable of cheapening herself by checking her own profile. The facade she creates is fully removed from her ego, cementing her heroic persona. Even as she becomes aware of the camera ("I am live on every screen in Panem," she notes in *The Hunger Games*), she is real, both to the viewers of the Games and readers of the Games, since by not watching herself she cannot be seduced into being what people want her to be. She can only be herself.

This trick has been pulled before by young people playing with American imagery. Kurt Cobain, the apotheosis of the reluctant media hero who came to power in the age of *The Real World*, made himself famous by being real, by being good, and by convincing the public that he did not care about his appearance. MTV pushed authenticity in large part by splashing Cobain across its screens; there were times in 1992 when "Smells Like Teen Spirit" was on television as much as the Hunger Games are on in Panem. When asked about the situation, Cobain had consistently ego-demolishing responses. (To a friend who remarked that he was on TV all the time, he said, "I don't have a TV in the car I live in."[4]) Although contemporaries report that he was as crafty and controlling of his media image as Katniss is of hers ("I pause a second, giving the cameras time to lock on me," she says as she slips out of a tree during the first Games), his suicide solidified his realness by erasing any chance of him slipping into a self-aware persona, and now he lives on as a saint of unadulterated artistry in a world that seems more artificial since his death.

Compare him to another rock star, Noel Gallagher of Oasis, who once said: "[B]eing famous is great. I love it, man. I think it's the best when you get stopped walking down the street for an autograph, that's the best feeling in the world."[5] A person who was truly busy being a heroic artist would not have time to be self-aware in such a manner. Whoops—Gallagher just checked his Facebook in front of everyone.

By the time *Mockingjay* begins, Katniss has gone from Cobain to Gallagher, fully aware of her image and struggling to maintain it. Asked to film propos—"propaganda spots;" wasn't Katniss *fighting* propaganda?—to support the rebellion, her prep team now "has to make me pretty and *then* damage, burn, and scar me in a more attractive way." Katniss' scars used to come from actual combat, unquestionably earned by her greatness; now they have to be rendered. Asked to say canned lines to inspire her followers, she suffers from stage fright; only when she is dropped into battle does she deliver inspirational speeches that are worthy of broadcast across Panem. Plutarch, Gamemaker and rebel leader, commends her spontaneity ("the audience eats that up,") even as

---

4. Charles Cross, *Heavier Than Heaven: A Biography of Kurt Cobain.*

5. "Oasis: What's the Story": http://www.musicfanclubs.org/oasis/act1.html.

he stages a wedding and dance in District 13, which normally holds neither, for the cameras.

Like many a hero and rock star before her, Katniss is trapped in her own persona. As early as the end of *The Hunger Games,* she has difficulty distinguishing between her real self—the girl who entered the arena—and the media powerhouse she has become: "I stare in the mirror as I try to remember who I am and who I am not." By the time she is filming propos as the face of the rebellion, others have noticed her confusion. "'I can't tell what's real anymore, and what's made up,'" says her lover Peeta, describing his confusion at who Katniss really is (*Mockingjay*). How can she escape? More than once, she considers the ultimate way, but when she sees herself shot on television, she inoculates herself against the escape hatch that lured Cobain.

Four years after my media training, I was given the chance to put Jessica's advice to the test on the *Today Show.* I was there to promote my second book, which had just been selected by the *Today Show* Book Club; it was the kind of pie-in-the-sky opportunity that authors get once if they are lucky.

I showed up early, as I was told was an absolute must. I went into the green room, which is never green, and saw the most unappetizing spread of donuts and fruit that I have ever seen to this day. It looked plastic, as fake as Katniss' propos. I sat in the room alone and watched the broadcast of the *Today Show* with the happy people on the street in New York behind the TV personalities waving signs. "Those are the people you aren't supposed to think about," I reminded myself. I was nervous, sick to my stomach. Jessica told me that the key with stage fright was to embrace it and convert it into energy. I tried, furrowing my brow and scrunching my guts. Soon enough I was called into makeup and then I stepped out under the lights to do the interview.

Like Katniss' talk with Caesar Flickerman, it was short. I sat up straight; I looked at the camera but did not look at the camera; I smiled. When I saw the tape later, I was dumbstruck.

How come no one ever told me that my mouth was so crooked? Why did I have my hair cut short so that I looked like a hedgehog? How was my head so skull-like? I seemed nervous, hyper, *self-aware*. I *was* self-aware. I could try and hide it through mental trickery and media training, but I had been self-aware the whole time I was getting ready for the interview and the whole time I was being interviewed. I am self-aware now, and barring a Buddha-like moment in middle or old age I will continue to be. I put the interview on YouTube, where it still resides,[6] but stayed away from television in the years that followed. I prefer email and phone. I prefer the control. I do not have the heroic, authentic persona necessary for TV.

Reading Katniss' interview in *The Hunger Games*, however, gave me hope that I was better than I thought. Before she goes on with Caesar, after she has been through her own media training, following the first question, when she is tongue-tied and about to ruin everything, Katniss thinks, *"Be honest."* This mantra, given her by Cinna after Haymitch's haywire advice, carries her through, and I, too was honest on the *Today Show.* I am honest now: I check my online persona regularly and am ashamed of it. I try to write and hope that people like it. I tried out for *The Real World* once and failed miserably. I was almost on *Queer Eye for the Straight Guy*, but the people in my building would not allow the camera crew. I play the games necessary to achieve success in my field. I have moments, like Katniss at the end of *The Hunger Games*, where I try to remember who I am and who I am not. I do not want to be famous for no reason . . . but I would take it. I can only hope the honesty of admitting these things outweighs the self-awareness of doing them.

Katniss ultimately reconciles her public profile with her real life by eliminating the former, leaving the Hunger Games and the rebellion behind to raise a family with Peeta. This is an act of self-denial that is unheroic for her public, but necessary for herself. The unadulterated heroism that she shows in the Hunger Games could only come out of a shining moment in youth, a time when she was firing on all cylinders; success brings reflection and reflection erases the authenticity that makes a modern hero. Transitioning to motherhood is a brave decision, both on Katniss' part and Suzanne Collins'.

At the end of *Mockingjay*, I was reminded of the Henry Hill monologue that closes *Goodfellas*: he says that after a lifetime of adventure, "I'm an average nobody. I get to live the rest of my life like a schnook." A schnook is not a hero. But Katniss is nothing if not a survivor. She does what she needs to to stay alive. And after she picks Peeta and retires from the public eye, into what spurious nest of lies does her other lover, Gale, go?

He goes back to District 2, to do television.

NED VIZZINI *is the author of three acclaimed young adult books:* It's Kind of a Funny Story *(now a major motion picture),* Be More Chill, and Teen Angst? Naaah . . . *Ned has spoken at over 200 schools, universities, and libraries around the world about writing and mental health. He writes about books in the* New York Times Book Review *and the* L Magazine. *His work has been translated into seven languages.*

PANEM ET CIRCENSES

▶

The Myth of the Real in Reality TV

CARRIE RYAN

We've tuned in to a lot of reality shows in the last decade or so, from the relatively harmless (*Dancing with the Stars*, *The Amazing Race*) to the somewhat more shameful (*Temptation Island*, *Jersey Shore*). We've watched, rapt, as contestants struggled to succeed and as relationships formed and fell apart. We've hung on every success, failure, and humiliation. But all of that is still a far cry from the Hunger Games . . . right? Carrie Ryan makes some troubling connections between reality television and the Hunger Games, and highlights just how fine the line between reality and fiction really is.

In the Hunger Games trilogy, Suzanne Collins takes our obsession with Reality TV and extends it to the most horrifying ends: a society that views kids killing kids as entertainment. It's easy to find this an uncomfortable premise—to turn our noses up and say that while we may enjoy *Survivor* or *Big Brother* every now and again, we'd never let society slip to such levels. However, there's also a deeper, more difficult message in the Hunger Games series: the extent to which media can be manipulated as a means of controlling the populace and how we as viewers have abdicated any agency in the process.

This then leads to an even more troubling aspect of the trilogy: our complicity in said message. But for the viewers' participation, the Hunger Games would not exist in the same way that, but for our tuning in, Reality TV wouldn't exist. By watching, we increase the ratings, and as our interest wanes the shows must become "more" to recapture our attention—more compelling, more extreme, more dangerous. And the only difference between us and the viewers in the Capitol is that we have agency to turn off the television at any time; we just choose not to. As Suzanne Collins shows us, the obsession with ratings, which is driven by our desire for more and more compelling narratives, can turn ugly when such a lens is applied to news reporting—especially that of war—rather than so-called Reality TV.

Ratings, Not Reality

With any television show, what matters are the ratings; getting enough people to tune in to make it economically worthwhile for the sponsors to pay for advertisements, which in turn feeds the ability of the show to keep filming. Reality TV is no exception. After 51.69 million viewers tuned in to watch the finale of the first season of *Survivor* in August 2000, the television industry realized that Reality TV could bring in ratings and turn a profit for a fraction of the cost of a fully scripted television show filled with professional actors. This started a trend that turned into a landslide, making the first decade of the twenty-first century one dominated by Reality TV. By the 2009–2010 television season, nine of the top twenty shows among young viewers were Reality shows.

For all its marketing advantages, though, Reality TV has to comply with some of the other basic rules of entertainment: to hold on to these viewers, the producers have to make each season fresh and new. In the absence of a script or predetermined plot, viewers would quickly get bored with simply watching a new group of people (or, in some cases, the same group of people) tossed into the same situation over and over again. Dealing with this problem largely translates into a perpetual upping of the ante, a constant raise of the stakes so viewers won't get bored.

Survivor is a key example. In the earlier seasons of the show, contestants brought a selection of clothes to the filming location, and the producers then chose what they could ultimately wear (camera-friendly colors, variety so not everyone wore the same thing, no logos). They were also sometimes allowed to bring a luxury item (such as when Colby brought a large Texas flag that he later used to help build a shelter), and the show provided necessities such as clean water, rice, and tools to build a fire.

Compare that to later seasons, where contestants were sent into the game wearing the clothes on their backs (whether that was a business suit or a sundress), weren't allowed any luxury items, had to hunt for their own water, and weren't provided food or any tools to make fire (though there were opportunities for teams to win these items at challenges—effectively inserting another level of competition for the base level resources that used to be a given). As the show grew and struggled to retain its dominance among the viewership, it became less about watching people live and scheme in a difficult environment and instead became about actual survival—the struggle of finding food, shelter, and water. In essence, the show became more brutal, and the driving force behind it all was the viewers—us.

The Hunger Games function the same way. Year after year, the Gamemakers struggle to make the Games appear fresh and new, crafting new arenas and devising new, increasingly sadistic challenges. What might one year be dense forests could in another be a vast arctic wasteland or a picturesque landscape filled with carnivorous squirrels or a dam that bursts, drowning half the tributes. The only criterion is that each year's arena has to outdo the one from the year before.

Ostensibly these machinations are intended to prove the power of the Capitol; however, a single, simple gladiatorial arena would have been sufficient to accomplish that. But while the Hunger Games are viewed as a punishment to those living in the Districts, in the Capitol they are entertainment and, as with any other reality show, the Capitol is concerned with ratings. Not for dollars, as in our world, but for something far more important: societal domination. The Games are symbolic of the Capitol's power and dominance: a boring game means the Capitol may appear weak and shy of resources in the eyes of its own citizens, who might then start to reconsider their allegiance to the Capitol they perceive as all-powerful.

Ultimately, as Plutarch points out in *Mockingjay*, the Capitol's main concern with the Hunger Games is providing *panem et circenses*: bread and circuses to keep the populace entertained enough that they won't consider rebellion. To do this, the Capitol continues to up the stakes, game after game. As Katniss realizes when the rules of the game shift again to pit her against Peeta at the end of the first Hunger Games, "They never intended to let us both live. This has all been devised by the Gamemakers to guarantee the most dramatic showdown in history" (*The Hunger Games*). Put another way: it's all about the ratings, and exploiting that very drive is what allows Katniss and Peeta to survive.

As Katniss and the leaders of the rebellion learn, if they want the citizens to revolt, they have to become Gamemakers themselves, appealing to those same sensibilities according to the same terms: presenting a compelling and entertaining narrative, not the truth.

Narrative, Not Truth

There's a famous line from the movie *The Usual Suspects*, where the narrator, Verbal, says of the enigmatic Keyser Soze, "The greatest trick the Devil ever pulled was convincing the world he didn't exist." To a certain extent the same quote, slightly modified, works for Reality TV: "the greatest trick Reality TV producers ever pulled was convincing the world what it's watching is real." Even the term Reality TV itself is part of the trick: it presumes Reality TV is an accurate representation of reality, when in actuality there is a difference between what is presented in these shows as reality and what most people would consider to be objective truth, which operates on several levels. (In recognition of this, there is a drive among some factions to change this to the somewhat more accurate "unscripted television.")

First, there are the truths presented by the Reality TV participants themselves to the viewer, to their editors, and to the other contestants, all of which may be different. Many Reality TV stars understand that there's a level of narrative construction necessary for strategic game play, both in terms of manipulating their fellow contestants and in terms of manipulating the ultimate viewer. In *Survivor: Pearl Islands* (the show's seventh season), for example, one of the castaways convinced the other members of his tribe that his grandmother had died so that they would give him the challenge reward. The castaway knew that by garnering sympathy, he could gain an advantage in the game, which worked. Not even the producers realized the castaway was lying until they called his home to offer their condolences, only to have the "deceased" grandmother answer the phone.

Lying about misfortune to garner sympathy is a tactic employed often in Reality TV, but the opposite is true as well: contestants regularly underplay skills or hide details about their personal lives if they feel it will give them an advantage (such as one housemate on *Big Brother 12* not admitting to being a doctor so that other contestants wouldn't feel like he didn't need the money). Katniss herself employed this tactic effectively in the original Hunger Games, concealing her skill with bow and arrow from the other contestants while using it to dazzle the judges.

Whatever the motivation, creating a compelling narrative is a sound strategy in winning a Reality TV show, especially one in which the recipients of that narrative—the viewers—can influence the game, whether through votes or by driving ratings. This has led to the ever-popular Reality TV romance—coined "showmance" by followers of the genre—which is compelling on-screen but evaporates as soon as the cameras turn off (one need only look to any of the bountiful subgenre of celebrity dating shows, and the fact that the same celebrities keep turning up for multiple seasons, to understand this). "Showmance" is at the heart of the Hunger Games, when Katniss and Peeta pretend to be a couple in order to influence the viewers' perception of them. As Haymitch explains after Katniss protests Peeta's declaration of love during the interview before the Games:

> Who cares? It's all a big show. It's all how you're perceived. The most I could say about you after your interview was that you were nice enough, although that in itself was a small miracle. Now I can say you're a heartbreaker. Oh, oh, oh, how the boys back home fall lovingly at your feet. Which do you think will get you more sponsors?" (*The Hunger Games*)

More important than the complicated truth of Katniss and Peeta's relationship is the idea that they could be in love. This creates a story that viewers crave and that they reward while the two tributes are fighting in the arena (and which readers rewarded by donning Team Peeta or Team Gale shirts while awaiting the conclusion to the trilogy to determine which bachelor Katniss would choose). This also made possible the ultimate act of rebellion: Katniss bargaining for both her and Peeta's life. Because viewers believe in and root for their love, the Gamemakers are able to save their reputation in the face of Katniss' rebellion.

This demonstrates a second break between reality and truth in Reality TV, perhaps even more manipulative than the first: how the editors and producers choose to present events. We like to believe that cameras do not lie, that what we see must be real because we have seen it. But contestants in Reality TV are often filmed a majority, if not all, of the day, which leads to thousands of hours of tape being edited down into a weekly show that may top out at twenty hours total over its full run. How editors choose to cut those tapes can change everything: they can choose to air only those few moments a day when contestants are complaining and make it look like that's all they do, or they can fail to air moments of contestants pitching in and make them appear lazy. Often, editors will craft a narrative stereotype of each contestant and show footage that backs up said stereotype: the loudmouth, the priss, the schemer, the layabout, the negotiator, etc.

And because many of the contracts between contestants and reality television shows explicitly allow the producers to have a hand in crafting the narrative, such interference is arguably within the bounds of what's acceptable and expected (in one extreme instance a former contestant on *Survivor* sued the show, claiming that they'd told other castaways how to vote; however, many Reality TV shows air a disclaimer that the producers have the right to consult on making decisions regarding elimina-tions). The post–reality show trauma ward is littered with former contestants who now say they actually got along quite well with the other contestant portrayed to the world as their nemesis.

Ultimately, editors and producers have not only the most power but also the most motivation to shape a narrative to bol-ster particular storylines. Sure, on some level perhaps these sto-rylines start out as organic truths, but reality is messy and complicated, and does not fit easily into preconceived arche-types or twenty-two episode seasons. Messy is hard to sell, so the editors give it a push, and ultimately these organic realities are twisted and enhanced to force them in the direction the editor believes will create the most compelling story.

For example, the truth of Katniss' threat to the Gamemakers when she and Peeta raise the poisoned berries at the end of the

Seventy-Fourth Games is that she's revolting against their rules and taking control of herself away from those who would use her. However, President Snow, as the ultimate producer of the Games, twists this to show not a rebel, but a "love-crazed school-girl" (*Catching Fire*). As Katniss realizes after the Games:

> Funny, in the arena, when I poured out all those berries, I was only thinking of outsmarting the Gamemakers, not how my actions would reflect on the Capitol. But the Hunger Games are their own weapon and you are not supposed to be able to defeat it. So now the Capitol will act as if they've been in control the whole time. As if they orchestrated the whole event, right down to the double suicide. (*The Hunger Games*)

The narrative constructed as strategy by Peeta and Haymitch becomes a sort of reality in and of itself, as Katniss begins to buy into it and President Snow capitalizes on it for his own ends.

Propaganda, Not Reporting

Collins, just like the Gamemakers in her books, raises the stakes to a new level in the third book of the trilogy, *Mockingjay*, when she takes the various themes of ratings and narrative and applies it to the way we approach reporting on wars. After all, it's not unexpected that the same viewership that craves an increase in drama from season to season of a Reality TV show would want the same out of war coverage. And it's not unsurprising to think that, in order to increase ratings, a television station or other news outlet might be tempted to construct narratives to corroborate the storyline they think will garner the most ratings. War coverage suffers from the same time constraints as reality television: every military front can't be shown at all times, and not even everything filmed can make it to air, which means things will always end up being left out. The result can be a story that, even if it's meant to be objective and accurate, is anything but. What gets chosen to be aired and what gets cut can have an enormous impact on the public's impression of war.

And sometimes editors determine what to cut and what to print in order to further their own agendas. For example, several historians have claimed that through his propensity for cherry-picking and sensationalizing details and publishing theory as fact, William Randolph Hearst and his *New York Journal* helped instigate the country's willingness to enter into the Spanish-American war in 1898. Behind the scenes of Hearst's reporting was a circulation battle he'd entered into with Joseph Pulitzer of *New York World*, and both recognized that the more sensational the headline, the higher the sales. Thus, much of their reporting wasn't about the reality of the events (it's acknowledged that most of their reporting came from biased third-hand information), but about what would increase circulation or ratings. Hearst and Pulitzer understood the truth that a well-crafted narrative can be beneficial for the bottom line, whether that bottom line is selling more newspapers, garnering more advertisers, or perpetuating a specific ideology.

This is never so evident as it is in *Mockingjay*, where Katniss is the symbol of the revolution, not through her actions, but through the carefully constructed and edited perceptions of those actions through propaganda. Even those moments that are based in truth, such as Katniss walking through the field hospital in District 8, are later molded into narratives. Shortly after visiting those same hospitals, Katniss and Gale engage in a battle with Capitol planes, after which Katniss becomes aware of the television cameras and shouts for the district to join the rebellion, essentially turning the moment into a commercial by taking that raw event and crafting it into a compelling bit of narrative about the war.

Katniss is always aware of the message her story sends and how those around her would like to control it for their own ends. As she explains: "They have a whole team of people to make me over, dress me, write my speeches, orchestrate my appearances . . . and all I have to do is play my part" (*Mockingjay*).

At each point, Katniss and the rebels are acutely aware of how their narrative will inspire the rebellion and how to take advantage of this fact. Cressida edits together moments from the Hunger Games and from Katniss' life as a series of propos designed to garner sympathy and loyalty for the Mockingjay, while Fulvia creates a series of *We Remember* propos about tributes lost to the brutality of the Capitol in previous Games. The Capitol engages in similar propaganda, having Peeta, once a symbol of the rebellion next to Katniss, publicly beg for a cease-fire in an attempt to temper the resistance. Both the rebels and the Capitol are engaged in a battle not just of soldiers but of narratives: editing moments together to elicit the desired response from viewers.

All of this culminates in the most dramatic and monstrous event in the book: the bombing of the children in front of the president's mansion in the Capitol's City Circle. It doesn't matter what the reality is behind the bombing, who conceived of it or ordered it, only how it is edited to shape the mindset of the people to finally end the war in favor of the rebels. And because this narrative fits into what we know of the Capitol already—that it is brutal and willing to kill twenty-three of its own children in the Hunger Games each year—we are willing to accept this atrocity as truth, regardless of who precipitated it. What matters is that the action is presented as truth and feels like truth. For many people, that's enough.

Real, Not Real

In his short story *How to Tell a True War Story*, Tim O'Brien writes that "a thing may happen and be a total lie; another thing may not happen and be truer than the truth." Sometimes a lie can get to the heart of a matter better than the truth, and sometimes a strict retelling of the truth cannot adequately capture reality. In this way, a trilogy like The Hunger Games, though it is fiction, can get to the truth of our obsession not just with Reality TV but with our willingness to abdicate our own responsibility in the face of what we're told is real.

Put simply: reality can be a lie. Narrators, producers, and editors can all manipulate those snippets of reality we watch, which can twist our perception of it in order to induce us to want more. And of course, if there's one thing we feel we can take as truth in these books it's Katniss and her narrative. But we should ask ourselves whether even this should be above suspicion. Like all first-person narrators, Katniss is her own editor with her own biases: she chooses how to present herself and those around her. Katniss has a stake in the story she's telling and what that stake is changes how she portrays the events and her emotional reaction to them.

Too often we accept what is labeled "reality" as truth rather than trying to understand what narrative the source might be promoting (whether that narrative is a quest for ratings or an attempt to promote a desired outcome). The Hunger Games trilogy demonstrates how an entire nation can be spurred into a rebellion through the use of propaganda and cleverly crafted narrative presented as reality. It shows how a culture's obsession with the dramatic, even if it is false, can lead to a complete abdication of personal responsibility in exchange for continued entertainment. We are responsible, as citizens, to look beyond *bread and circuses* and not to accept information as it is handed to us but to search for a deeper truth.

We can rail against the dominance of Reality TV shows, but so long as viewers continue to watch them, advertisers will continue to sponsor them and they'll keep being produced. This is the true nature of the industry. In the end, if there is one truth that can be taken away from the Hunger Games it is this: we, the reader, tuned in and boosted its rating. Even while Katniss rails against the Games as disgusting and barbaric, we the readers turn the pages in order to watch them. We become the citizens in the Capitol, glued to the television, ensuring there will be another Game the following year. Thanks to us, the ratings are just too high to cancel the show.

CARRIE RYAN *is the* New York Times *bestselling author of several critically acclaimed novels, including* The Forest of Hands and Teeth, The Dead Tossed Waves, *and* The Dark and Hollow Places. *Her first novel was chosen as a Best Books for Young Adults by the American Library Association, named to the 2010 New York Public Library Stuff for the Teen Age List, and selected as a Best of the Best Books by the Chicago Public Library. A former litigator, Carrie now writes full-time and lives with her husband, two fat cats, and one large dog in Charlotte, North Carolina. You can find her online at www.carrieryan.com.*

NOT SO WEIRD SCIENCE

▶

Why Tracker Jackers and Other Mutts Might Be Coming Soon to a Lab Near You

CARA LOCKWOOD

Part of the pleasure of reading the Hunger Games is how alien its world is: the names, the food, the way people live. However dark the story becomes, reading about Panem is always laced with the excitement of discovery. Even mutts, some of Suzanne Collins' scariest creations, seem thrilling just because they're so strange. But as with all the best science fiction, Katniss' world has more in common with ours than we might initially think. Real-world scientists aren't far from being able to create mutts of their own. Here, Cara Lockwood explores genetic splicing, the dangers of technology in both worlds, and the responsibility that comes with creation.

I will admit right now that I am entirely too critical of most sci-fi. I'm the one sitting in the movie theater grumbling, "that could never happen." Or, more concisely, I'll just say: "Seriously?"

Could there be some crazy disease somewhere in a lab that would turn the entire planet into brain-eating zombies or sunlight-fearing vampires? No way. Beefing up shark brains to make them super-smart predators? I don't think so. Crazed prehistoric-sized piranhas that will devour anybody with an inflatable floatie and a cooler? Please. They want us to believe this stuff?

Like take the insane DNA-spliced mutant monsters that make terrifying cameos throughout the Hunger Games. I'm supposed to believe that one day we could be ripped apart by mutant wolves with tribute eyes? Stung by poisonous and relentless tracker jackers? Or get devoured by giant lizard men?

Seriously?

As it turns out . . . maybe so.

Not only do muttations—"mutts" for short—already exist in our world, but the stuff real scientists are doing is far wackier and sometimes scarier than what we see in the Hunger Games—if you can imagine that.

In this essay, you'll read about some of the movie-worthy stuff going on in labs right now that makes jabberjays seem quaint. We'll talk about why real-life sci-fi is way scarier than anything you might find in the Hunger Games, and about the lesson we can learn from Panem about not playing God and using science wisely.

But first: let's talk about the science that makes mutts possible: genetic engineering.

Could Tracker Jackers Exist?

In the real world, genetic engineering—the science of altering DNA by adding or subtracting genes in order to create a different kind of creature, or in some cases the science of cloning an existing one—isn't new. In 1997, scientists in the United Kingdom reproduced the first genetically cloned sheep, named Dolly. Dolly was simply a duplication of a sheep's embryo—a clone—implanted into a different sheep and brought to term like a normal sheep.

You may have heard of Dolly, but did you know that another sheep was actually genetically engineered with some human genes fused into the DNA of the sheep? CNN reported the news later in 1997 shortly after the new sheep, named Polly, was born and before many countries passed laws banning experiments using human DNA. So, yes, technically, we've already had a human-sheep hybrid. Of course, we aren't talking about an unusually furry guy named Bob who can produce the wool to make his own argyle sweaters. While a human-sheep hybrid *sounds* pretty creepy, these post-Polly hybrids looked like sheep; they only had a few human genes among tens of thousands.

And we didn't stop with sheep.

In 2001, American scientists genetically spliced a jellyfish gene into a moth, making a new moth designed to kill the pink bollworm—a pest that destroys cotton crops. Jellyfish and moths? It sounds exactly like something you'd find in the Games.

But genetic engineering gets weirder.

Scientists have been working on genetically engineering silkworms that could spin silk strong enough to repel bullets by
splicing silkworms and spiders. By weight, spider-silk could be
stronger than steel and tougher than man-made fibers used in a
soldier's body armor.

Gene splicing is pretty much what it sounds like. You cut
into the DNA of a gene to add some new stuff—except you
don't use a knife. You use chemicals—certain enzymes that will
"cut" into the DNA strand. Then scientists add in new DNA
and glue it all back together with another enzyme. Since DNA
is what makes a cell a cell and determines its function, the splice
in DNA causes changes—like the production of extra-strong
spider silk or pink bollworm poison. And, there you have it, the
beginning of our very own mutts

One day we could even be eating nothing but mutts.

The New Scientist in July reported that scientists have already
engineered pigs with omega-3 fatty acids. So forget bacon and
eggs—you might be able to get all your nutrients straight
from the bacon. They're also working on cows immune to
BSE, or mad-cow disease, and a host of other engineered animals, including faster-growing salmon that could be on our
dinner tables faster than you can swim upstream. And unless
you live in Europe, where there are stricter laws governing
genetically engineered foods, nearly every kind of vegetable or
grain you eat is already genetically engineered.[1] From toma-
toes that stay ripe longer to green peppers and zucchini that
are resistant to viruses and pests to rice that contains more
Vitamin A, most of our crops are genetically engineered in
some way.

---

1. See "Altered animals: Creatures with bonus features" in *New Scientist*,
July 2010.

So, we're working on some seriously crazy stuff. Some possible super dystopian sci-fi Panem stuff. (I might have to stop saying "seriously?" at the movies and start taking the possibility of a shark/squid hybrid or a time-traveling hot tub, actually, well—seriously.)

It's a Mad, Mad . . . Scientist

At first glance, it certainly seems like there's a big difference between our genetic engineering and Panem's. Mutts are dreamt up in Capitol labs and designed to wreck havoc on the tributes at the Games, plus pretty much anybody daring to stand up to President Snow or his regime.

They're terrifying. They're unnatural. They're bloodthirsty and murderous. They attack without warning, and they don't stop until their victim is dead. They devour, slash, and rip apart the living. In the sewers in the Capitol, Katniss Everdeen flees a lizard mutant:

> For the first time, I get a good look at them. A mix of human and lizard and who knows what else . . . Hissing, shrieking my name now, as their bodies contort in rage. Lashing out with tails and claws, taking huge chunks of one another or their own bodies with wide, lathered mouths, driven mad by their need to destroy me. (*Mockingjay*)

These aren't just predators, they're actually *driven mad* by the need to kill. They work themselves into a frenzy, like sharks when there's blood in the water, except that even sharks eventually stop killing. Mutts never do—no matter how much they eat.

"No mutt is good," Katniss says in *Mockingjay*. And let's face it. Science can be scary. It's no accident that the mad scientist is an enduring villain who creeps up at every Halloween party. Mad, ego-driven, over-confident scientists have been the bad guys in everything from Mary Shelley's *Frankenstein* to the crazy gene-splicing madman in *The Island of Dr. Moreau* and the well-meaning but over-reaching scientist couple in *Splice*. The idea that science can lead to the unnatural creation of monsters isn't new to the Hunger Games, and it's easy to take that to mean science is, well, evil.

Let's look at what else Katniss says in *Mockingjay* about mutts:

> No mutt is good. All are meant to damage you . . . However, the true atrocities, the most frightening, incorporate a perverse psychological twist designed to terrify the victim. The sight of the wolf mutts with the dead tributes' eyes. The sound of the jabberjays replicating Prim's tortured screams. The smell of Snow's roses mixed in with the victims' blood.

The killer mutts are terrifying, but it's not because of science. The Gamemakers and the scientists designed them to scare the stuffing out of you. That's why they are such effective weapons. It's not just that they're unnatural; it's that they're created specifically to get inside your head and stay there. If mutts are bad, it's not because science is bad. It's because the people who created them are.

After all, not *all* science in Panem is bad. There's an upside to science—even in Panem.

Take Peeta. The Capitol's scientists torture him to near insanity using tracker jacker venom, but then Beetee—the most scientific of the tributes (Katniss calls him a smart inventor who "could tell by sight that a force field had been put up" in *Catching Fire*)—Prim, and the other doctors and scientists in

District 13 help Peeta recover using similarly scientific anti-brainwashing techniques. And the very technology that brings tracker jackers and killer monkeys to life in the arena ultimately saves Katniss' life when she finds herself desperately wounded by an explosion during the last rebellion battle in the Capitol. She's engulfed in flame, but genetically modified skin grafts help her walk and move again. Science saves her life.

After, Katniss refers to herself as a mutt, but it's clear that just by receiving the treatment she hasn't turned into some killing machine, like the lizard monsters that chased her through the sewers. She's the same Katniss she always was.

So—we have the very same technology in Panem being used for very different things. It can be used to create monsters or to save lives.

Science is only a tool; it's how you use it that matters.

Which means that if we just use our science for good, then we're in the clear, right? I mean, as long as we create things with *good* intentions, then we'll never create an evil, bloodthirsty monster. Then—presto!—science is good and everybody wins. Right?

Maybe you already see where I'm going with this.

The Path to Muttdom is Paved with Good Intentions

Scientists in our world and in Panem often develop new inventions with the desire to help us, but what either intends isn't always what ends up happening.

Once you create a new technology, even with the best of intentions, you can't always control how it's used or what the consequences are. The rebel forces of District 13 fall prey to this.

When Gale helps the rebels develop new weapons in *Mockingjay* with the idea of saving lives in the districts and righting past wrongs, they end up killing a member of Katniss' family, a tragedy he'd hadn't foreseen and would never have wanted. He is the one who helps Beetee come up with the plans for the bomb that is later used to kill Prim: a bomb with one explosion that kills the soldiers and then a second, delayed explosion targeting the rescue workers who come to help them. Gale's hand in developing this weapon, whether it was the rebellion's bomb that killed Prim or not, costs him Katniss' love.

That's the problem with developing weapons in particular. Even weapons you hope will advocate the "good" cause might be turned against you—or maybe even the very people you're trying the hardest to protect.

And think about real world science. We're developing genetic mutts right now with the very best of intentions—to cure disease, help people live longer, grow more food so less people go hungry. It's all noble, good stuff.

But every new scientific development is like opening Pandora's Box: it's not just the good stuff that comes out. In July 2010, another scientist took a quantum leap forward. He didn't just splice together the DNA of animals that already exist—he actually created a completely artificial cell. Doctor and researcher Craig Venter created an entirely new life form by making a man-made DNA code and named the cell "Synthia." Venter believes this new artificial cell could be the key to solving all sorts of problems—cancer, disease itself, you name it. But other scientists don't think Synthia is a good thing at all. They think that a completely synthetic cell, not bound by the rules of nature and millions of years of evolution, might actually pose a threat to every life form on the planet, including ours. Such a synthetic creation, they say, wouldn't play by the same rules as normal life. Bacteria and viruses have actually lived with us for thousands, if not millions, of years. They've evolved to live with us, and we've evolved to live with them—even though they sometimes kill some of us. A life form not bound by all those years of a symbiotic relationship might just kill everything by accident. In fact, it could bring on a plague like the one seen in the movie *I Am Legend* that nearly wiped out the human race.[2]

Seriously.

So, with the path our own scientists are on, maybe we end up curing cancer. Or maybe we accidentally make a synthetic virus that ends up killing most of the world's population. Maybe both. It sure seems like a roll of the dice. No matter what our intentions are.

Unforeseen Consequences

The fact is, while human beings are pretty smart when it comes to figuring things out like genomes and genetic cloning, sometimes we're pretty dumb about more basic things, like the consequences of our inventions. Our overconfidence in our own abilities can often lead us to bad places, because we fail to predict what our inventions will actually *do*.

It's the Frankenstein problem. If you get all fixated on the creation of something without thinking it through, you're probably going to miss some fairly important and obvious consequences (like 1. if you make a monster he will need some guidance/love/parentage from you, even if you're too scared or

---

2. See "Scientist accused of playing God after creating artificial life by making designer microbe from scratch, but could it destroy humanity?" in *The Daily Mail*, July 2010.

grossed out to give it; 2. a neglected monster is a ticked off monster; and 3. ticked off/rejected monsters have trouble assimilating into society and more than likely will end up killing people). Ergo, instead of being hailed as the world's greatest scientist, you wind up creating a monster that doesn't do what you want it to do and ends up rampaging through the countryside getting chased by a bunch of ticked off torch-and-pitchfork-wielding villagers.

The Frankenstein problem happens often to the scientists of the Capitol. When they made jabberjays—exclusive male homing birds designed to mimic entire human conversations as a means of spying on rebels—their living spy equipment was soon turned against them, as rebels learned to use the birds to their advantage. And while they were never intended to survive on their own (that's why they were all male, so the Capitol would be able to control the jabberjay population), the jabberjays ended up mating with mockingbirds in the wild, creating mockingjays.

The mockingjay winds up becoming a symbol of all that the Capitol *can't* do. That's why it becomes the symbol of the rebellion. Mockingjays are a living symbol of the Capitol's shortsightedness and proves that it isn't invincible. That despite all its technological and scientific advances, it makes mistakes just like anyone else. That makes it vulnerable. The Capitol learns the hard way that the more it tries to control both the districts and nature itself, the less control it actually has.

The Games themselves are a perfect example of this, as well. The technological advances that make the Hunger Games possible—the vast technology that creates the arenas, the mutts that make up the obstacles, and the scientific know-how from people like head Gamemaker Plutarch—all of these things were designed to keep the districts in line through fear and intimidation. And yet, rather than keeping everyone in line, the Games make some people in the Capitol eager to rebel. Plutarch and Cinna and others secretly work for a rebel cause, undermining President Snow's power. Snow can't see that the Games—designed to control the people in the districts—actually undermine his own control over the people in his own Capitol, leading to a complete unraveling of the entire government.

Snow was equally short-sighted when it came to his own health. In his desperate grab for power, he used science (chemistry, specifically) to kill people—with poison. But, there are consequences he hadn't foreseen. Snow drank poison "from the . . . cup himself to deflect suspicion. But antidotes don't always work. They say that's why he wears the roses that reek of perfume. They say it's to cover the scent of blood from the mouth sores that will never heal" (*Mockingjay*).

Because Snow's problem wasn't just that he hadn't thought things through—he had been overconfident in what science could do for him and how well the antidotes would work. That overconfidence, more than anything, can be our downfall. We sometimes look to science to fix all of our problems. We *assume* it can. After all, science has a great track record—we've developed vaccines, clean drinking water, indoor plumbing. Biology and physics have made our lives longer, healthier, and easier. We've grown to think that science can fix nearly anything, but it can't. Sometimes, science just creates new problems.

In the Hunger Games, as in many sci-fi cautionary tales, there's a lesson to be learned from tragic overconfidence in science. We may think we've got it all figured out, but we just can't foresee every eventual consequence of our new inventions.

So, What Now?

To use science responsibly, we need to 1. apply it with good intentions; 2. go slowly so we can try to think out every possible consequence for our new inventions; 3. don't get too cocky; and 4. understand that science can cure problems *and* create them—usually at the same time.

Sounds like a tall order. But the alternative is even more bleak. If we stopped scientific research altogether, we might as well just head on back to the pre-Newton dark ages. Dying of an infected paper cut doesn't really sound like a great way to go, if you ask me.

We have to go forward; there's just no way of knowing whether we're doing the right thing as we go.

That's why they call it "playing" God—because we aren't, actually, God. Even with the best of intentions, science can lead us down a path of self-destruction. *That's* why it's such a good bad guy in movies. That's why—even in our world—it makes such a nice scapegoat.

The answers aren't easy. Scientists argue with each other constantly about what makes ethical research and what doesn't. The best we can hope for is that we at least *try* to be good and that we don't look blindly to science to solve all our problems.

But perhaps the most valuable lesson of all is that the harder we work to control nature, the less control we actually have. As much as we'd like to control everything, we just can't do it.

It's just like quantum mechanics. Everything looks neat and orderly in our world until you get to the atomic level, and then you realize it's just a bunch of subatomic particles bouncing around. In a word: chaos.

So we can go forward with our inventions in genetic engineering cautiously and with thoughtfulness, or we can make the same overconfident mistakes that so many of the Capitol scientists made in Panem.

In short, science isn't evil, but it isn't a cure-all, either. As long as we understand our own limitations—that we aren't, in fact, God—maybe we can avoid Panem's fate.

Let's hope that—like Katniss—we make the right decisions, even when they're not easy to make.

And here's hoping that wasp's nest I just found near my back door is not the genetically engineered tracker jacker kind.

Seriously.

CARA LOCKWOOD *writes for teens and adults and has written nine novels in several genres. She created the Bard Academy series, about a reform boarding school haunted by famous authors and their fictional characters. The series includes* Wuthering High, The Scarlet Letterman, *and* Moby Clique. *She lives in Chicago with her two daughters and is working on her next book. Visit her at www. caralockwood.com or www.bardacademy.com.*

CRIME OF FASHION

TERRI CLARK

For readers with a passion for fashion (or a good makeover), the passages where the outfits Cinna designs for Katniss are described in meticulous detail are some of the most enjoyable parts of the Hunger Games. For readers without such interests—and Katniss herself—they may feel more like torture. If you've been skipping over these pages, though, you're missing out on one of the most important themes in the series. Great fashion, Terri Clark points out, does more than look good in the Hunger Games trilogy: it saves Katniss' life, and sparks a rebellion. As Peeta says to Tigris in *Mockingjay*, "Never underestimate the power of a brilliant stylist."

Dress shabbily and they remember the dress; dress impeccably and they remember the woman.

—Coco Chanel

B y its very definition, "fashion statement" means our clothes speak for us. When a person thinks of that phrase, they are most likely to picture someone whose conscientious choice of attire stands out and evokes a strong response. Right now, Lady Gaga is the poster child for making provocative fashion statements. Who else would don a raw meat dress designed by Franc Fernandez and say it was in protest of the Don't Ask, Don't Tell policy? Yet, if she yanked on a pair of tattered sweats and a Hanes t-shirt among friends in the privacy of her own home, that too would articulate something about her. Because even when we're not trying to draw focus to ourselves, what we choose to wear *still* makes a statement.

Our clothing tells other people who we are, whether we value comfort over frivolity, brand names over money-saving knock-offs, timeless styles over trendy couture, loud patterns over the invisibility muted colors offer. Look at Katniss when we first meet her. She normally dresses in trousers and a shirt, her hair braided beneath a cap, with supple leather hunting boots molded to her feet. Kat's unintentional fashion statement is one of practicality and function. She doesn't care about what she wears past its usefulness, because she is too concerned with survival. Her clothes reflect these values, and what has made them necessary, including her low social status and her frequent hunting expeditions. That she wears her father's old hunting jacket communicates her love for him and his influence on her life. Like it or not, what we dress in is a direct reflection of who we are personally, socially, and historically.

Sometimes, though, we make a conscientious decision to use our attire to convey a certain image or message to others. Muslim women demonstrate their religion by wearing hijabs, scarves that cover the head, ears, and throat. A recent high school graduate might proudly exhibit his college acceptance by wearing a Dartmouth sweatshirt. A teen girl can shout her allegiance by wearing a Team Jacob t-shirt and a man can tell everyone who he's rooting for in the Super Bowl with his Denver Broncos ball cap.

And of course, sometimes, we choose to convey an image that isn't true. A fifty-something woman can wear low-cut jeans and a cropped top to look younger while she trolls the clubs. A man can put lifts in his shoes to appear taller. A young actress can stuff her bra to get a director's attention. Every day, in a million ways, we share information about ourselves, whether true or false, through our appearance.

No one better understands the philosophy of fashion than Suzanne Collins' fictional character, Cinna. All of the Capitol stylists are well practiced at polishing and presenting their contestants, but Cinna takes this craft to a new level. Not only is he genius at creating provocative, memorable costumes, he utilizes his fashion artistry as a political platform that subtly plays on his audience's sensibilities. He gives the people of Panem a heroine to root for, plucks at their romantic heartstrings, and fires up their indignity over injustice, and he does it all through fabric.

Thanks to this gifted and courageous designer, Katniss Everdeen heralds her arrival to the Hunger Games in stunning, unrivaled fashion and exits, as its most controversial winner, with equal power and aplomb.

Initial Spark

We know Katniss' understated stylist, whose only concession to personal modification is metallic gold eyeliner that compliments the like-colored flecks in his green eyes, actually chose District 12 for his debut as a designer. From the start he had an image in mind for the humble huntress. He would turn her into . . . the girl on fire.

Perhaps Cinna was inspired by the first impression the nation receives of Katniss as a brave young woman, dressed up for the reaping in her mother's hand-me-down, soft blue dress and matching shoes, willing to sacrifice herself to keep her younger sister Prim safe. It had been decades since someone in District 12 dared to volunteer him or herself as a tribute, but Kat's fierce surrender and her district's silent salute to her fearlessness and singularity awes viewers from the outset.

It is customary for the Capitol stylists to create costumes for the contestants that, as Cinna says, "reflect the flavor of the district" (*The Hunger Games*): agriculture for District 11, fishing for District 4, and factories for District 3. In past years stylists had taken the coal-mining angle for District 12 and tried to make it sexy. Unfortunately, for the opening ceremony, this meant creating skimpy outfits with headlamps or, the very worst, having the contestants completely nude except for black body powder used to represent coal dust. Fortunately, Cinna is an out-of-the-box thinker and takes the traditional coal dust/miner angle one step further. What do you do with coal? You burn it. The theme of Cinna's makeover for Kat during the Games is based first on this idea and then later on the small golden mockingjay pin she wears as a token. Fire becomes symbolic of District 12, including Peeta, but the mockingjay belongs to Katniss alone.

Of course, we've seen the power of fashion outside of fiction. In 2000, a certain Bronx-born singer/actress, who wasn't well known at the time, made viewers gasp in admiration and abhorrence at the Emmys when she wore crystal-encrusted panties beneath a plunging, leaves-little-to-the-imagination, sheer chiffon jungle print Versace dress, magically held together by a single jeweled pin just below her navel. Jennifer Lopez might've lost Best Dance Recording to Cher that night, but it wasn't *Believe* everyone spoke about after. It was J-Lo.

By donning that one "look at me, remember me, root for me" dress she became an overnight sensation. Pictures of her flooded the internet and were plastered on the front page of every magazine. At the water cooler, people dared to wonder how she kept the dress on, while the *Today Show*'s Matt Lauer and *South Park*'s Trey Parker spoofed her cutting-edge couture by donning copies. The infamous garment has even garnered a spot in Los Angeles' Grammy Museum. Like Troy Patterson said in his "Best of 2000: Rock Frock" article for *Entertainment Weekly*, "She turned herself out as the fly girl hyperversion of postfeminist power, flaunting her control by toying with the threat of excess. In consequence, her star went supernova." Without question, the dress cemented Lopez in the cultural consciousness and allowed her to strut out of the Bronx, break social barriers, and step through previously barred doors. Ultimately, one dress told the world, "I may have come from nothing, but I'm something now."

Kat's metamorphosis first begins with her being mercilessly waxed, tweezed, scrubbed, and polished before donning what she calls "either the most sensational or the deadliest costume in the opening ceremonies" (*The Hunger Games*). The simple black neck-to-ankle unitard and knee-high shiny leather boots are a silent contrast to the vibrant, fluttering cape and headpiece ablaze with red, orange, and yellow streams. Cinna also makes a deliberate choice to keep her face fresh of makeup, with her hair braided in its signature style, so she is recognizable to the audience as that brave girl from District Twelve. When Katniss and Peeta finally ride out on their chariot, colorful capes and headdresses burning with synthetic fire, their faces are illuminated by the dazzling flames. Stylistically it is a stunning first impression that captures the crowd with its "look at me, remember me, root for me" daring.

From the get-go it is Cinna's intention to curry audience favor and thereby increase the couple's chance of survival through sponsorships. His audacious opening-ceremony outfits tell the audience these are two fiery competitors to be reckoned with. Combine that with his unprecedented directive for the rival contestants to hold hands and demonstrate a united front, and he accomplishes his goal by literally burning Kat and Peeta into viewers' memories, while establishing them as a couple and creating an instantaneous fan following. At the same time, he brilliantly makes his mark as a debut designer by managing to do what other stylists couldn't: he makes District 12 look electrifying and mighty instead of grimy and ineffectual. It's during his couple's singular introduction to the crowd that we realize Cinna's no ordinary stylist and fashion can be a powerful force to be reckoned with.

Fanning the Flames

Once Cinna turns the spotlight on Kat, he has to keep it there. With that in mind, he carefully designs a look for her pre-game interview that invokes power, while still highlighting her girlish attributes. Fire has long been a symbol of destruction, purification, illumination, and change, and Cinna appears to recognize these imposing qualities in his young charge, even when she does not. President Snow later tells Kat, "Your stylist turned out to be prophetic in his wardrobe choice. Katniss Everdeen, the girl who was on fire, you have provided a spark that, left unattended, may grow to an inferno that destroys Panem" (*Catching Fire*).

To make certain the rest of the world sees what Cinna does, he gives every last detail of Kat's interview look a defining touch. Flame-painted nails, stenciled skin, artfully braided hair, huge dark eyes, full red lips, and shimmery gold skin complement his dress of jeweled flames. Reflective gems of red, yellow, white, and blue give the impression Kat is "engulfed in tongues of fire" when she gives a flirty twirl (*The Hunger Games*). From her fierce cosmetics to the flame theme that's carried through from fingernails to skirt, Cinna suggests to the audience that Kat is strong enough to withstand the heat of competition. The craftmanship of his outfit inspires oohs and aahs amongst the spectators, while Kat's honest charm wins their hearts. In the end, she is "made beautiful by Cinna's hands, desirable by Peeta's confession, tragic by circumstance, and by all accounts, unforgettable" (*The Hunger Games*). It is the perfect way to begin the Hunger Games.

Flashover

In an irony that couldn't have been foreseen (except, of course, by Suzanne Collins), the competition becomes as monumental as Cinna's designs—demanding attention, pushing boundaries, and forever changing the future. When Kat defiantly divides a handful of poison berries between her and Peeta, denying the Capitol's desire for a solitary champion, her ingenious ploy forces the Gamemakers to announce two

victors in the Seventy-fourth Hunger Games. Her civil dis-
obedience makes her a rebel hero in Panem, while branding
her a political enemy of the Capitol.

Cinna's primary strategy for Kat's survival up to this point
has been about gaining favor for her as a contestant, but at the
close of the Games her inimitable spirit and refusal to bow
before the government means Cinna must find a way to protect
her from President Snow's wrath. So what's a spunky girl supposed to do in her post-game interview after she's survived, but
become the enemy of her nation's leader? Why, act the demure,
vulnerable lady, of course.

This certainly isn't a new strategy. Hul-lo, celebrity court.
Courtney Love, Paris Hilton, Nicole Ritchie, Lil' Kim, Lindsay
Lohan—any number of female celebs have cleaned up their acts
and traded in their titillating attire for demure suits and good
girl decorum when called before a judge. The fun-sized singer,
Lil' Kim, was especially known for her provocative, outrageous
fashion choices: itty-bitty, pink cashmere bikini, orange plastic
superhero suit, and most famously, her skintight purple pant-
suit by designer Misa Hylton-Brim, which left one breast bare
except for a seashell pastie and motivated Motown legend Diana
Ross to cop a feel, on the air, during the 1999 VMAs. Yet, when
Lil' Kim was indicted for perjury, conspiracy, and obstruction of
justice, she showed up in court looking chic and reserved in a
khaki pant suit, tailored jacket, and charcoal skirt. It was an
attempt to persuade the judge and jury she was more than the
provocative persona she put on for the cameras and deserved a
break. Her conservative courtroom clothes clearly contradicted
her public image. Did her attempt to change people's perceptions of her by cleaning up her appearance work? Not so much.
The diminutive diva served ten months in jail.

Next take Lindsay Lohan and her many, many, maaany court-room visits. This trash mag queen has always tried to tame her image with classy clothes. In July 2010, when she appeared in court for violating her probation, she actually changed her outfit THREE times during the one-day hearing! Her final outfit, a black cowl-necked jumpsuit, modest white cardigan, and peep-toe platform heels, did little to dissuade the judge from sentencing her to ninety days in jail. Really, it's a shame LiLo's stylist, assuming she had one, didn't have Cinna's attention to detail or she might've noticed the expletive painted on her client's sherbet-colored fingernails and prevented the fashion faux-pas that made international news and almost got Lindsay a contempt of court charge. Clothes might make the woman, but it takes long-term remodeling to permanently change an unfavorable impression. Otherwise you're just putting lipstick on a pig and hoping its snout looks smaller.

Fortunately for Katniss, Cinna knows just how to present his champion for her crowning and she doesn't have an established reputation with her audience as a bad girl to overcome. In a calculated move that temporarily confuses Kat, her stylist skips sophistication for soft, innocent beauty. From Kat's flat leather sandals and loose hair to her clear-polished nails and seemingly simple yellow dress, Cinna creates the image of a tender, harmless girl. The stylist, knowing what grave danger Kat has inadvertently placed herself in, presents her as a sweet innocent child who is as far from a political revolutionary as possible. At the same time Cinna gives the audience, who has come to love her, a girl who is a direct, relatable reflection of it: someone just trying to do her best under terrible circumstances, someone who has suffered great loss, someone who dares to hope for love and a brighter future. The sheer fabric of

Kat's magical dress glows softly like candlelight, reminding everyone she is still the girl on fire but giving her a more delicate, non-threatening edge. The golden glow also adds a romantic touch as Kat and Peeta, hands entwined, watch their tragic love story unfold onscreen with the rest of Panem. For Kat's final television interview with Caesar, Cinna sticks with the same theme of angelic simplicity and dresses her in a gauzy white dress and pink shoes.

Her softened image further instills her in viewers' hearts but, like the real-life celebrities we've discussed, her fashion about-face does little to sway the person who most matters. President Snow isn't affected by her fashionable plea for mercy in the least, nor would Cinna expect him to be. But because Cinna has done his job so well and the audience clearly adores Kat, Snow chooses to bide his time.

The Fire Spreads

Back in District 12, Kat toggles back and forth between wearing her preferred hunting gear and Cinna's clothes, which her mother believes are more appropriate to her status, but as Kat heads out on the Victory Tour she is once again placed at the mercy of her stylist and his team.

During the tour, she sees her mockingjay emblem, her token from the first Games, everywhere. Katniss' pin, which depicts the bird in flight connected to a ring by its wingtips, mocks the Capitol. As the unintended offspring of the Capitol's genetically enhanced jabberjays and wild mockingbirds, the mockingjay is a symbol of strength, adaptability, and triumph over oppression, the perfect representation of the bold and defiant District 12 tribute.

It's also the perfect representation of a nation ready for change, and after Katniss wins the Games, the little bird adorns belt buckles, watches, silk lapels, tattoos, and more. Some likely wear the symbol only because it is associated with their heroine. For others, however, it shows they've joined the rebellion. Unlike most other fads—Snooki's poof, I <3 Boobies tees, and Silly Bandz—the mockingjay trend holds a powerful message of political solidarity. The public tells Kat, "We're behind you. We believe in you. We're ready to follow, and continue what you started."

When Katniss is forced to return to the arena for the Quarter Quell, she knows Snow plans to get rid of her. Once again, Cinna steps in to make a fashion statement. Kat's opening ceremony outfit is meant as a warning to the President. Despite his wishes, Kat will not go quietly; Snow shouldn't underestimate her a second time, and the other tributes should fear her. To convey Kat's indomitable strength Cinna bypasses the softer touches and subtle messages in her opening ceremony outfit. Her makeup is dark and shadowed and her fitted black jumpsuit glows like burning embers. The pièce de résistance is a crown, marking her as a victor, which burns an angry red. Seeing herself in a mirror, she thinks, "Katniss, the girl on fire, has left behind her flickering flames and bejeweled gowns and soft candlelight frocks. She is as deadly as fire itself" (*Catching Fire*).

Initially Cinna's designs are meant to capture the audience's attention and turn them into avid Kat supporters. Further down the line, the importance of that goal intensifies as Kat's involvement in the Games turns political in nature. When it comes to melding fashion with politics, no one better understands the power clothes hold than Michelle Obama and Sarah Palin.

Fashion insiders analyzed, criticized, and praised their campaign wardrobes the way pundits did the candidates' views on hot

button issues. Obama was praised for wearing youthful, afford-
able designers. By staying away from the staid, conservative look
so many first ladies bow to, she not only looked spectacular, she
seemed a tad rebellious for bucking the age-old tradition in a
way that also complemented her husband's message of change.
On the other side of the runway, Palin was crucified in the media
for her exorbitantly priced attire. From her rimless glasses to her
designer power suits, her carefully constructed image was meant
to project smarts and strength, marking her as a worthy running
mate for John "Maverick" McCain. Instead, her lavish threads
marred the small-town, "Joe Six-pack" everywoman reputation
she'd tried hard to cultivate. After all, how many average American women can afford to spend $150,000 on clothes? For both
ladies, matching their clothes to their message was the difference between success and failure, and their outfits spoke louder
than words.

After the Quarter Quell announcement and a few weeks
before the Games begin, Cinna has the foresight to design a
black uniform that Kat describes as being "at first glance
utterly utilitarian, at second a work of art" (*Mockingjay*). The
carefully crafted outfit keeps Kat safe with its layers of body
armor and reinforcement over her heart, but the precise tai-
loring, swoop of the helmet, curve of the breastplate, peek-a-
boo sleeves, and hidden weaponry make this final outfit by
Cinna starkly attractive as well. But the most important outfit
Cinna designs in his short career, the one that propels Panem
into rebellion and signs his death warrant, is Katniss' Quarter
Quell interview outfit.

Coco Chanel once said, "In fashion, you know you have succeeded when there is an element of upset." Cinna more than
succeeded with his greatest creation. When the victors give
their pre-game interviews to Caesar for the Seventy-fifth Games,

many of them voice their upset at being chosen to compete again. Their heartfelt pleas wreck the crowd. Then comes Kat's turn. Dressed in her bridal gown as dictated by President Snow, she tells the audience she's so sorry they won't be able to watch her wedding, but she's pleased she can, at the very least, share the dress with them—a dress that, unbeknownst to Kat, Cinna has secretly modified. The white silk gown with floor-length sleeves and millions of pearls was voted on by the people of Panem. Now it stands as a tragic, romantic symbol of star-crossed lovers who will never have their happily ever after, a frilly testament to wishes never fulfilled, a painful reminder to every Panemian of what they too have lost. As the audience contemplates her sad fate, Katniss begins to twirl and her dress catches fire! She spins faster and faster as smoke and flames engulf her. Pearls clatter to the floor, silk darkens and burns away. When she finally stops turning, the dress has been transformed. The design is the same as her wedding gown, but Kat now stands covered in coal-colored feathers. Her draping sleeves resemble wings, her veil a crown of down. She stands before the audience as a beautiful mockingjay. The ultimate symbol of resistance. Without words, Cinna fans the spark of defiance Kat's single act of insurgence in the first Games lit in the districts. Her fiery transformation from broken bride to mighty mockingjay is a call to arms, a battle cry for independence, and a stand against oppression. With lace and feathers, pearls and veil, a war is begun.

"Don't worry," Cinna tells Kat in *Catching Fire*, fully knowing what he has done and what it will cost him. "I always channel my emotions into my work. That way I don't hurt anyone but myself."

Despite the danger his daring design places him in, Cinna makes his voice heard. Perhaps writer Eric Hoffer said it best when discussing creativity, "Discontent is at the root of the creative process . . . the most gifted members of the human species are at their creative best when they cannot have their way, and must compensate for what they miss by realizing and cultivating their capacities and talents." Discontent with the Capitol leads Cinna to commit a crime of fashion. Without question it also brings about his creative best. Through his work he helps rid the world of Snow's dictatorship, and like many renegades, he dies for his cause. In the end, Kat shouldn't be given all the credit for starting the revolt. She might be the flame, but Cinna is the torch.

TERRI CLARK *feels blessed to demonstrate her passion for young adult fiction as both a teen librarian and author. For as long as she can remember she's been fascinated with the paranormal, so it's little wonder her stories are a bit edgy and twisted.* Sleepless *(HarperTeen) is about a teen who is stalked in her dreams by a killer and her short story in the* Breaking Up Is Hard to Do *(HoughtonMifflin) anthology delves into mind-reading. Terri was also a contributor to the non-fiction anthology* Flirtin' with the Monster *(BenBella Books). Her next paranormal,* Hollyweird *(Flux), will be released in 2012. You can visit Terri online at www.TerriClarkBooks.com and at www.facebook.com/terriclarkbooks.*

BENT, SHATTERED, AND MENDED

▶

Wounded Minds in the Hunger Games

BLYTHE WOOLSTON

The Hunger Games series is littered with characters who have experienced severe physical and mental trauma, from Katniss' mother to Haymitch and the other Hunger Games victors to Katniss herself. No one ever uses the term Post-Traumatic Stress Disorder, but, says Blythe Woolston, the indicators are all there. Woolston explains how PTSD works, why the design of the Hunger Games makes the disorder almost inevitable for those who survive it, and how Katniss, Peeta, and the others may eventually be able to heal.

The Hunger Games trilogy gave me bad dreams. Actually, the books provided images, feelings, and ideas that my brain used as ingredients to brew up nightmares about children's bones floating in a river of red dust and creepy lizard mutts lurking in the storm drain outside my front door. My brain is good at that sort of thing. But dreaming wasn't the only business my brain was doing while I slept. It was also forming memories. That is why I remember Greasy Sae's concoction of mouse meat and pig entrails, Prim's untucked shirt, and, of course, Katniss, the girl on fire.

You probably remember why Katniss called Prim "little duck." It's a detail that's important to the story. But—unless you share my personal fascination with mice and nasty-bad soup—Sae's recipe isn't stashed in long-term memory. That's because every individual has a unique brain in charge of selecting information and forming memories. Depending on our previous experiences, we notice some things and ignore others. In the process, we build an ever-more-specialized system for dealing with the world. We can donate a kidney or a chunk of liver or a pint of blood to someone else and those cells have a good chance of being useful, but the brain and the memories in it can't be transplanted. Brains are weird, custom-made, do-it-yourself projects.

The Hunger Games is an especially good series to read with the brain in mind. Nightmares, memories, and hallucinations are an important part of the story—and all of those things are brain business. Why does Katniss behave as she does? I think the answer to that question depends upon understanding her brain, not her heart. In order to understand Katniss and her choices, we have to understand how a brain makes sense of the world and what happens to a brain when it's plunged into the senseless world of the Games arena.

We'll start with brain building, focusing on the way the new-born brain makes sense of the self, the physical world, and the social environment. With that foundation, we can look at the way memory happens, both in normal situations and in trau-matic circumstances. The Hunger Games is a frightening expe-rience that bends, breaks, and shatters minds. When we look at the tributes individually, their behaviors reflect the damage done. Finally, we can look at healing, the ways that damaged minds might mend—at the way that Katniss and Peeta move forward at the conclusion of the book.

Building a Brain

Compared to the heart, which is pumping like a pro before the umbilical cord is cut, the brain is a late bloomer. A new-born heart can move blood all the way to a baby's hand, but that hand won't be under meaningful control by the brain for weeks or months—maybe years. Forging the brain/body con-nections required to become an expert archer like Katniss is a project beyond most of us at any age, but even walking, something most of us *can* do without conscious effort, requires an impressive network of nerves to relay sensory inputs and responses.

Delayed development isn't the only way that the brain differs from the rest of the body. Bones or muscles have to *add* cells to mature, but the maturing brain *subtracts* cells, weeding out an overabundance of neurons. The result is an ever-more efficient network. Scientists refer to this process as pruning.

This "less is more" approach also drives the brain's first encounters with the world. It has to sift through a "blooming, buzzing confusion" of sensory impressions.[1] If you take a moment to notice all the things you usually don't—like the pressure of clothing against your skin, the multitude of hums and whispers in the air, and the motionless things at the edge of your peripheral vision—you realize that awareness is as much about deciding what can safely be ignored as paying attention to useful kernels of information.

Babies are dedicated researchers, and the world is their laboratory. An infant begins by discovering the self, making the connection between mind and body—essentially learning to use the equipment. It takes trial and error to discover how to do complicated tasks like focusing the eyes and "finding" the hands. Once the hands and eyes are coordinated, exploration of the physical world progresses rapidly. Splashing around in a bath provides information about the nature of water and the power of the body to move things. Chucking a toy to the floor is an excellent test of gravity, and, after gravity has been proven reliable, it becomes a social experiment. How many times will someone pick it up and give it back? All of this activity is about discovering the self, the physical environment, and the social world. Once that foundation is laid, learning new things and responding in creative ways to new situations becomes possible—as long as we have a system to store and access experiences. That system is memory.

---

1. Psychologist William James came up with this description in 1890. It's hard to do any better.

Memory Happens

Cells throughout the body communicate with each other, but brain cells have an extraordinary ability to reach out and form connections—they make thousands upon thousands of links with other cells. When you learn something, when you make a new memory, there is always a change in the connections. But memory is something the brain *does*, something that happens, not something that just *is*. Memory isn't something that sits around in a single brain cell waiting to be useful like a spoon in a drawer. When a memory pops into your head it means a specific web of interconnected brain cells has been activated and all those neurons are in communication with each other.

Brain cells, like all cells, communicate chemically, and some of the most powerful chemicals that affect brain cells are those that help us respond to danger. It wouldn't matter what other fancy things the brain could do if it didn't have some skills useful for keeping us alive. It needs to recognize danger and figure out how to avoid it. Remembering which berries are poisonous can mean the difference between life and death. We evaluate the present and future based on memories of past experience. When we learn, the brain remodels, building corresponding networks of connections among cells.

We have control over some of the memories we build. Studying is basically all about making memories on purpose. If you repeatedly think about *myomancy*, which means foretelling the future by observing the behavior of mice, you will be able to access that memory and use it. (Although a future where knowledge about myomancy is a practical skill is hard to imagine.) There are other memories that happen without study. These involuntary memories are often tied to exciting, unexpected events in life—like waking up to find a mouse walking across your face. If that happens, you are likely to experience a flood of chemicals that makes your heart race *and* excites your brain. The moment you felt mouse toenails on your eyelid is a moment you'll remember, whether you want to or not. Mice can be startling, and that kind of surprise sets chemicals coursing through the brain that cause very strong connections to form *without* repetition. You only need one frightening encounter to learn to be wary of a situation that might cause you harm. That's handy, since repeated exposure to potential dangers is—well—dangerous.

If you end up seeing mice or feeling little mouse feet in your dreams, that's a sign the experience has made a cozy nest in your neurons. Although science doesn't know the exact mechanisms, there seems to be a connection between dreaming and building lasting, accessible memories. Not every experience is dream-worthy, and not everything we see or do or discover ends up in long-term memory, either.

Two things seem necessary for experiences to be successfully stored in long-term memory. First, the connections the experience forms between networked cells must be strong and enduring. The network needs to be in place for potential reactivation so the memory can "happen" in the brain. Second, the memory must undergo a process called "consolidation." Dreams may be tools we use to sift through the day's new memory networks and "consolidate" them. The brain, after all, is still just trying to make sense of all those experiences. Making narratives is a way to make sense of events, and dreams might just be efforts to tell a story, to put the pieces together.

That's the way memory works when things are "normal." But the world the brain lives in isn't always safe and secure. Some surprises—a serious injury to your body or witnessing a bloody accident—are far more horrific than a mouse. It isn't easy to integrate those shocking experiences with other memories. Sometimes fear doesn't fade, and instead of a single wash of chemicals to help build quick, strong connections, the brain experiences wave after wave of them. There is no time for the brain to rest, to sort through the networks, and make sense of what has happened. Sometimes the world is more like the Hunger Games.

Wounded Brains

"There are still moments when he clutches the back of a chair and hangs on until the flashbacks are over. I wake screaming from nightmares of mutts and lost children."

—from *Mockingjay*

The horrors of the bloodbath at the Cornucopia may take only seconds, but the memories formed in those seconds are permanent—and painful. When the brain remembers them later, the flood of chemicals that usually makes quick reactions possible instead swamps the brain. Until the fear subsides, those chemicals dominate how the brain works. Memory networks activate, flashing like strobe lights, growing stronger and stronger, creating a feedback loop of fear and sensations. When a brain is having that sort of trouble, a specific set of symptoms emerges: nightmares, flashbacks, emotional numbness, violent outbursts. These are symptoms of PTSD (Post-Traumatic Stress Disorder). These are also torments that Katniss Everdeen and the other tributes suffer after living through the trauma of the Hunger Games.

The symptoms of PTSD fall into three different categories.

Memory-Related Problems

A memory created by a terrified brain is often very active, very powerful, and very difficult to consolidate with other memories. Such a memory is like a chainsaw that suddenly appears in your living room. It might be a useful thing to have, but you don't really know where to put it. The chainsaw is for cutting things, but it doesn't belong in the silverware drawer with the steak knives. It doesn't belong in the refrigerator or on the bookshelf. So you leave it on the stairs until you can figure out what to do with it. That's a problem. The chainsaw is in the way. It intrudes. Sometimes you trip over it and it hurts. Worst of all, sometimes it roars into action without warning, threatening everything, including you.

Living with a "chainsaw" memory is intense. As the brain struggles to "learn" and store the memory, recurring nightmares can happen. Fear, real fear, bubbles up in reaction to the nightmare, which just makes the memory stronger. Everyday sensations—a smell, a flashing light—can be linked to the original, horrifying experience and become "triggers"[2] that evoke vivid involuntary memories called flashbacks. Flashbacks don't seem like a memory. They feel real. The brain relives the memory as a present, frightening reality. For Katniss, Snow's white roses are a powerful trigger. Their unmistakable bioengineered scent is strongly linked to her encounters with him. To smell that perfume, the mingling of blood and flowers, is to be in his presence. That is why Snow leaves the rose in the vase for Katniss to find after she returns to District 12. He knows that he has forged a connection and built a trigger that will make her afraid.

---

2. We all have memory "triggers," but most of our memories are not intrusive and painful. The smell of car wax might remind you of a summer afternoon with your big brother, or a bite of licorice could send you zooming back in time to the day you learned to tie your shoes.

Avoidance

Avoidance is a basic response to pain. It's fundamental. Bees sting: avoid bees. Similarly, when a trigger sets off a painful memory, avoiding the trigger seems like a logical response. But avoiding bees may also mean eliminating roses, dandelions, and even honey from your life. That's a lot of beauty and sweetness sacrificed.

There is another sort of avoidance that carries a much higher price: emotional numbing. Here again, the logic is simple. If you can't feel it, it can't hurt you. But numbing-out dulls all emotions, not just the unpleasant ones. Katniss' mother provides an early example of this emotional shutdown and its consequences. To avoid emotional pain after the mine explosion, she becomes so numbed and withdrawn she is unavailable to her daughters. Blunting sorrow means blunting happiness, and dodging grief means dodging love. Katniss is angry with her mother, but she is also learning from her example. One of the very first things Katniss reveals about herself is that she is determined never to marry, never to have children, because she can't imagine a future where those children will be safe from the reaping. Even before she is made a tribute, Katniss has been hurt by the Games. She, like many children who suffer from PTSD, has a foreshortened sense of the future. She expects the worst because, so far, the worst has happened. That is why Gale can't be more than a hunting partner—ever. Katniss will lay down her life to defend children already in the world, like her sister Prim and Gale's little sister Posy, but she won't give the world any more hostages. She is willing to give up a world of love if it means she can avoid a world of hurt.

Hyperawareness

In a dangerous world, it is important to pay attention. It's worth taking time to look both ways before you cross the street. It's worth watching where you put your feet when you hike in rattlesnake country. When the tornado siren sounds, it's good to seek shelter. But a traumatic experience can mess with your internal controls. Every moment feels like you are stuck in the middle of a busy street while a tornado full of rattlesnakes is headed your way. It doesn't feel safe to ignore the multitude of hums and whispers in the air or the motionless things at the edge of your peripheral vision. To a nervous system on constant "red alert," danger is lurking everywhere—all the time.

If you want a little taste of the difference between normal awareness and hyperawareness, scrape your knuckles against a cheese grater, then pour lemon juice on the cuts. Ordinarily, your skin protects those nerves. A brain that is functioning normally is similarly protected. But for the hyperaware brain, there is no protection, no barrier between it and the world. Everything—every tiny noise and every innocent touch on the shoulder—is like lemon juice in a cut. You can't ignore it. It all hurts. It all might mean something, and what it probably means is that you are in danger.

Sleep is impossible. It's hard to concentrate or learn because the brain doesn't have the opportunity to consolidate any new memories. It's much too busy dealing with the constant onslaught of data. Lashing out is a natural, if unwarranted, response. Hyperawareness messes with the mind as much as tracker jacker venom.

The environment of fear damages the brains of the tributes—and even the audience watching the events unfold on television. It isn't accidental. The Games are instruments of terror and control. The lotteries, the lavish preparations for the spectacles, and the catastrophes in the arena are all fine-tuned by the Gamemakers. When we look at the tributes who survive, there can be no question that the long-term ruin of their lives is as deliberate as the uniform height of the flames of an unnatural forest fire.

Bent, Broken, and Shattered: The Survivors of the Hunger Games

. . . a lot of them are so damaged that my natural instinct would be to protect them.

—from *Catching Fire*

Haymitch Abernathy, the first surviving tribute we meet, is a clownish, snarling boozehound who has to be hauled away on a stretcher after taking a header off the stage. He doesn't inspire much confidence. Both Katniss and Peeta know him as the town drunk, but as Effie Trinket scolds, while hopping pointy toed through Haymitch's vomit, he is their only lifeline. His mentoring can make the difference between life and death. Surely Haymitch knows that, and surely no one could be so selfish that getting staggering drunk could seem more important than making at least a *little* effort to save a life.

Self-medicating with alcohol—or "morphling" for that matter—is common among people suffering from PTSD. Alcohol is a depressant that blunts anxiety and fights insomnia. Narcotics have a similar appeal. Haymitch isn't a drunk because he has plenty of money and nothing better to do. He is a drunk because he lived through a Quarter Quell. He held his own intestines in his hands while he witnessed his would-be murderer brained with an ax. Then, every year for twenty-four years, he has been reminded of that experience, made to relive the help-lessness and horror as he watched children from his hometown suffer and die. Haymitch drinks because he has PTSD and has no other way to treat his symptoms. And he isn't alone.

The Quarter Quell tributes are all suffering from damage done by the Games. Some, like Peeta and Beetee, have obvious physical injuries. The symptoms of PTSD are just as obvious. Disassocia-tion of mind and body, difficulty speaking, anxiety, avoidance, and nightmares—those are injuries caused by traumatic experi-ence. It isn't a coincidence. The Games are a well-designed instru-ment of terror, and the lasting damage they inflict on the survivors is one of their most important functions. When the victors return home, they are still a weapon in the Hunger Games. Living trib-utes, like Haymitch, are "rewarded" with new status and even a new home, and isolated not only by their relative wealth, but because neither they nor anyone else can forget that their fellow tribute did not return. The victors are walking reminders of ter-rible communal loss. The spectacle may be "entertainment" for the citizens in the Capitol, but it is traumatic for those who live in the districts. They are required to watch, helpless, while their child or friend is murdered on the static-filled screen, and they live with daily reminders of the outcome.

Remember all that brain-building work? The Hunger Games demolish it. They tear down the self, create a physical world where the rules don't apply, and shred the fabric of social rela-tionships. The participants are, first of all, reclassified—they are "tributes," not people. The self is disembodied and packaged as an image observed on a television screen. In the arena, the phys-ical world is so manipulated that everything is untrustworthy. Butterflies have poisonous stings, and blood falls in suffocating storms from the sky. Finally, the most fundamental social agreements, like mutual cooperation and the taboo against murder, are violated.

Disintegration of the Self: Losing the Body

They erase my face with a layer of pale makeup and draw my features back out.

—from *The Hunger Games*

Grooming, even when it involves a "full polish" that removes three layers of skin, may seem like the least of the tributes' problems. Ditto being costumed in velvet and jewels. But the pageantry does more than improve the production qualities of the "entertainment" for the capitol audience. There is an underlying message that cuts deep. The message is simple: a tribute is not a person. It is a body, nothing but property to be toyed with, destroyed, or sold.

Finnick Odair knows this. As he reveals to Katniss, he, the most beautiful of the living tributes, has been prostituted by President Snow for years. He didn't choose promiscuity and casual sexual encounters for his own pleasure; he has been sold to the highest bidder. The price for refusing would be the death of the defenseless Annie, the one person Finnick loves. By definition, Finnick has been raped, forced into sexual intercourse against his will. Rape is a traumatic violation and a common cause of PTSD. Dissociation of the mind from the body is a defensive response to it. It allows Finnick to remain functional, rational, apparently in control. But when Annie is in peril during the rebellion, this bargain between mind and body collapses and Finnick disintegrates into the depression, distraction, and difficulty concentrating associated with PTSD.

Another sign of the broken link between mind and body is the loss of meaningful speech seen among the tributes. Unlike the speechlessness of the Avoxes, whose tongues have been cut out as punishment, the strange speech patterns of the Quarter Quell tributes originate in the brain.

Both Annie and Wiress drop out of conversation in mid-sentence. Annie drifts off and "laughs at odd places in the conversation." When Annie "does that thing where she covers her ears and exits reality," it is part of her own pattern of avoidance and disassociation (*Mockingjay*). Annie lapses in and out of connection when a loud sound or other trigger makes the present as painful as the past. Wiress also has speech problems. Her behavior is different than Annie's, though. She is easily "distracted by something in her head" or a bit of dry straw (*Catching Fire*). Beetee acts as her translator. He knows her well enough to finish her unfinished ideas. It probably took years for the two of them to share that sort of connection, but it only takes a few minutes in the bloodbath at the Cornucopia to steal away all of her language but two syllables: "Tick, tock." It is a heroic effort at communication, one that saves the lives of her allies once they understand her message. It is also clear evidence that her extraordinary, creative, intuitive brain is still struggling to work—"nuts" or no. And then there is Old Mags, whose garbled speech may be the result of a stroke as Katniss speculates, but who might be suffering from aphasia, the inability to recall words. It's a frustrating aspect of the "swiss-cheese brain" that plagues people with PTSD—they know exactly what they want to say, but the words seem to have been erased. Katniss, for her part, falls completely silent after the death of Prim. She is a mental Avox.

It isn't the first time that the connection between mind and body has been broken inside Katniss. When she wakes after Rue's death, basic tasks now require conscious effort and attention. She

isn't exactly herself anymore; instead she is telling some girl
named Katniss what to do: "I give myself a series of simple commands to follow, like 'Now you have to sit up, Katniss. Now
you have to drink water, Katniss.' I act on the orders with slow,
robotic motions" (*The Hunger Games*). Later, when she must
watch the highlights of the Games, seeing herself causes Katniss
to disassociate again. "Something inside me shuts down and I'm
too numb to feel anything. It's like watching complete strangers
in another Hunger Games" (*The Hunger Games*).

The Arena: Insecurity in an Undependable World

*It's not an aggressive move, really, but after the arena, I react
defensively to any unfamiliar touch.*

—from *Mockingjay*

Natural disasters like tsunamis, hurricanes, or earthquakes are
unexpected catastrophes. It is impossible, really, to be psychologically prepared for events that suddenly upend the world and
leave a tangle of death and wreckage behind. Homes are reduced
to rubble, and even the landscape may be unrecognizable. Those
who live thorough the immediate devastation are stranded in a
hostile environment where nothing feels safe or secure anymore.
It's all too much to process. As a result, many disaster survivors
experience anxiety, nightmares, and other symptoms of PTSD.

The arena for the Hunger Games is a carefully designed
unnatural disaster. Orchestrated wildfires, avalanches, and floods
all add to the stress and carnage of the Games. In the arena, the
mist that creeps through the jungle at night is nerve gas, and
the perfume that rises from the flowers is poisonous. Even
gravity is suspended, so a rock thrown over a cliff flies back up,

untethered by natural laws. Nothing in the environment is dependable. The earth underfoot can suddenly spin so fast the centrifugal force flings bodies through the air.

The arena is populated with nightmare versions of real animals: fluffy little squirrels are carnivorous pack animals, monkeys have claws like switchblades, and the birds' songs echo the screams of tortured children. Clearly being dangerous isn't enough to merit inclusion in the Games. If it were, the arena would be crawling with pit vipers and rattlesnakes. Psychological horror is as important as poison. A pack of wild dogs can kill you, but a muttation that stares at you with the beautiful emerald eyes of a dead girl? Worse. Much worse.

There is no safe place. Fear is constant, and, in response, the brain shifts to a hyper-aroused state and gets stuck there. As Peeta says, "The pink sky and the monsters in the jungle and the tributes who want your blood become your final reality" (*Mockingjay*). When that happens, it is very difficult to trust the world ever again. The whole world *is* the arena. Even if gravity is reliable and "the Games" are over, the brain has been taught that safety and security are illusions.

The Social World: "I don't want it to come down to you and me."

> . . . *I don't know what to tell him about the aftermath of killing a person. About how they never leave you.*
>
> —from *Mockingjay*

That brain-building baby, long before it learns to talk, also has things to teach us about how deeply embedded we are in a social world. I find one experiment especially revealing.[3] Babies between the ages of six and ten months watch a puppet show where distinct geometric shapes play the roles of "climber," "helper," and "hinderer." When the little red circle tries to climb a steep hill, it can't do it. Then a blue square arrives and "helps" by pushing the circle to the top. In the next scene, a yellow triangle appears and, instead of helping, blocks the way and shoves the circle to the bottom of the hill. At the end of the show, when the babies have access to the puppets, they reach out to touch the pro-social blue square and shun the yellow triangle.

This experiment reveals how quickly a brain recognizes a difference between "good" and "bad" behaviors and how deeply we desire to be allies with "helpers."

Consider what that means in the arena. Alliances form, but they must dissolve because, as Maysilee Donner tells Haymitch, "I don't want it to come down to you and me." The Games are designed that way, designed to push the tributes to cross the line from ally to murderer.

How did that line come to exist? Why are most humans so reluctant to kill another human being? What is the real difference between killing a deer or squirrel and "murder" from the brain's perspective?

Some of it may be instinctive; most mammals exhibit a resistance to killing members of their own species. (There are exceptions to the rule—usually triggered by hunger or the desire to reproduce.) The reluctance to kill other humans might also be a result of socialization, part of the whole package of learning to

3. See J. K. Hamlin, K. Wynn, & P. Bloom's "Social evaluation by preverbal infants," published in *Nature*, Nov 22, 2007.

depend on others as an infant. Whatever the origins, the evidence that killing takes a psychological toll is clear. The most obvious data comes from a study done of soldiers who had all lived through war. Even though all members of the group shared similar experiences of threat to life and witnessing deaths of others, those who knew that they had killed another human being during battle were far more likely to develop symptoms of PTSD. The brain finds killing another human being traumatic.[4]

In fact, overcoming the resistance to kill other humans is one of the primary functions of military training. Simulations and other preparation that help a soldier react quickly and pull the trigger rather than hesitate are an advantage on the battlefield. Similarly, the Career tributes step into the arena with an edge over the others. Their greater physical training plays a minor role compared to the power of the psychological training that makes them willing to be the aggressors.

Sometimes training works too well. Titus, a tribute from District 2, got over the taboo against murder and became good at killing. Then he turned cannibal. That was too much for the Capitol—and the home audience—to accept. Titus was wiped out of the game with a well-timed avalanche. The line that can't be crossed is very subtle. It is, apparently, socially acceptable for Enobaria to tear out another tribute's throat with her teeth— teeth she later has sharpened and inlaid with gold—but actually eating the flesh of the dead is forbidden.

Katniss, the hunter, has had more experience with death than most. She knows how to kill. She also knows that there is a difference between hunting and murder. Despite having a weapon

---

4. See Maguen, et al.'s "The Impact of Direct and Indirect Killing on Mental Health Symptoms in Iraq War Veterans" published in *Journal of Traumatic Stress*, February 2010.

and expertise, she avoids directly taking a life as long as she can. Only after Rue is attacked does Katniss shoot the boy from District 1. Later Katniss' brain replays the events and she considers what it means. He was her first kill, the first person she knew would die because that is what she intended. The act of launching the arrow is not much different than the many times she has done it while hunting, but she knows a truth about murder, about killing another human being. She knows what Peeta says later, "It costs everything you are" (*Mockingjay*). Katniss draws the bowstring back. The arrow finds its mark. The boy from District 1 is dead, and even though Katniss doesn't know *why* she should care about that boy, when her brain replays the events of the day she sees not only Rue's death over and over again, she also sees her arrow piercing the boy's neck. She thinks about his family, weeping for him. She wonders if he had a girlfriend who loved him and hoped he would return. No matter what the circumstances, killing that boy is difficult for Katniss' brain to accept. Whether her reaction is rooted in instinct or culture, the result is significant trauma.

Mending

It takes ten times as long to put yourself back together as it does to fall apart.

—from *Mockingjay*

At the end of *Mockingjay*, Katniss has been moved far from the center of attention, flown away and settled in a virtually vacant District 12. The post-rebellion world, where both Snow and his potential successor Coin have been scrubbed from the picture, doesn't need Katniss. She is an uncomfortable memory.

She was essential during the rebellion, but she isn't any longer. The world just wants to forget, and as long as Katniss is there, they can't. So she is hidden away where she won't trigger painful memories for those who are trying to build a new world. She doesn't fit into the new narrative, the new stories they will make for themselves. Those stories might include heroic figures like the girl on fire or the Mockingjay, but a broken young woman who finds life almost unbearable? No. The real Katniss won't be part of that story. Her story is different. It is a story of slow healing and small comforts.

Even in this imaginary future, it is easier to break than it is to mend. The Capitol has the technical ability to poison a mind with traumatic, false memories. That is how they hijacked Peeta and turned him into a weapon to use against Katniss. The opposite treatment, the ability to remove a painful memory with chemical or technical means, doesn't seem to be part of the medical knowledge in the Hunger Games world. Peeta has to sort through his memories, both false and true and decide what to believe.

In the here and now, we are still trying to crack the puzzle of PTSD. Recently, researchers at Johns Hopkins announced that they could erase traumatic memories by removing a protein from the brain—in mice.[5] That's huge, but it doesn't help Peeta or Katniss or any real-world sufferers of PTSD. We are very far away from having an easy fix for the problem.

So how can what is broken be mended? Can Katniss recover from the damage done? The short answer is that she will never be the same. She will never be the person she might have been if she hadn't been traumatized. The stress, the loss, the shock:

---

5. Always with the mice . . . Seriously, the progress in memory research is astonishing. While I was writing this essay, several major breakthroughs were announced.

There is no undoing that, just as there is no way to save Prim or Rue. Katniss may always struggle with nightmares. A trigger might surprise her and set off a memory she wants to forget. But it is possible to move forward, and Katniss is doing that as well as she is able.

Peeta shows us one path to recovery: He paints. He recreates the scenes of horror that haunt his dreams. It may seem contradictory to focus on those images instead of trying to ignore them. Katniss certainly feels that way when she says, "All I do is go around trying to forget the arena and you've brought it back to life" (*Catching Fire*). Still, Peeta really is on to something. His own nightmares haven't stopped, but when he holds the brush in his hand, when he paints, he is in control of the images. He may not erase them from his memory, but he can tell his story through painting. He's working through the process of moving those images from the place in his brain devoted to emotion—particularly fear—and shifting them to other places of his brain. It doesn't happen fast, but his paintings are a way to move forward. Expressing the story is an opportunity to reshape reality, to rebuild it. The hand holding the brush does what the brain wants. Mind and body grow back together. Once the memory is shifted out of the place of fear, it is less likely to escape and intrude into every waking moment.

Most of the progress is a small comfort, like the bit of rope that passes from Finnick to Katniss to Peeta. The key is to focus on this moment, the present. It may be nothing more than a distraction at first, that bit of rope, but it is so dependable. It is there. It is real. And it helps. Your favorite color is green and mine is orange. You always tie your shoelaces in a double knot. Those are the tiny things that are real. Knowing those little truths is a place to start to build the world over again—and relearn how to trust it.

Memory triggers become less dangerous. A primrose can be planted as an intentional reminder, a memorial. Dandelions bloom where fire blackened everything. Good memories are like that, small and persistent. That's why Katniss gives her attention to every act of goodness she has seen. She really is like the mockingjay. In the past she was an instrument, a weapon in a war, but life is finding a way forward in her. It's a long way back, but in a safe place, with a few people who love her without demanding heroics, she is finally able to trust the world enough to have children and make the book that remembers all the things that should not be forgotten. She's imagining a future. That takes more courage than being a girl on fire.

BLYTHE WOOLSTON *is the author of* The Freak Observer, *a novel about coping with PTSD (no, really, it's about theoretical physics and grief . . .). Her second book, which is about learning to live with the scars of a MRSA infection (no, really, it's a buddy road-trip novel with lots of trout fishing . . .) is scheduled for release by Carolrhoda Lab in February 2012. She lives mostly in Montana. She conducts her virtual existence at BlytheWoolston.com.*

THE POLITICS OF MOCKINGJAY

▶

SARAH DARER LITTMAN

Reality television wasn't the only inspiration for the Hunger Games. Television news during the War on Terror also played a role. And news coverage is something Sarah Darer Littman knows well. She isn't just a YA writer; she's also a newspaper columnist whose political column ran during the height of the war. Here, she uses her experiences to draw some alarming parallels between war in Panem and in our world that may change the way you think about not just Presidents Snow and Coin, but also Peeta, Gale, and even Katniss.

aybe it's because of my political background, but when I read Suzanne Collins' Hunger Games series the focus was never about Team Gale or Team Peeta the way it was for so many readers; the romance was a subplot. I majored in political science in college, and when I'm not writing books for teens, I'm a columnist for Hearst newspapers and a writer and blogger for various political websites, including CT News Junkie and My Left Nutmeg. To my mind, the Hunger Games trilogy was always more about "The System"—a political system that would not just allow but *require* children to fight to the death in televised games.

According to an interview in the *School Library Journal*, Collins said she drew her inspiration for the Hunger Games from imagining a cross between the war in Iraq and reality TV, after flipping through the channels one night and seeing the juxtaposition between the coverage of the war and reality TV programming. While I've never had the privilege of meeting Suzanne Collins and have no idea as to her political views, I don't think that the uncanny similarity between the themes she took on in *Mockingjay* and the issues that we as a nation struggled with during the Bush administration's War on Terror is an accident.

Reading *Mockingjay*, I relived through Katniss some of the helplessness, frustration, anger, and confusion that I felt during the eight years of the Bush administration—the same sense of looking at my country Through the Looking Glass that I continue to feel when I see certain religions and ethnic groups being demonized by politicians and media figures. I experienced that same helplessness I felt when I read about American citizens being designated as "enemy combatants" and held for years without the right of *habeas corpus*. The same anger that coursed through my veins when I read that our government was using waterboarding, a recognized form of torture for which we prosecuted Japanese officers after World War II, yet using the Orwellian doublespeak of *"enhanced interrogation techniques"* in an attempt to desensitize us to this departure from both our national values and international law. Perhaps this is why this book has stuck with me and buzzed around my brain for months after reading it.

This dark period of our history has particular resonance for me because it was during the years when I was cutting my teeth as a regular political columnist for the *Greenwich Time*. I started in January 2003, on eve of the Iraq war. It was, perhaps, an inauspicious time to be a critic of the Bush administration in the predominantly Republican town of Greenwich, Connecticut, where George H.W. Bush had grown up and the Bush family still has roots. One of my early columns, entitled "Bush in a China Shop," warned that the administration's failure to secure broad-based support for the Iraq war didn't bode well for any subsequent peace and quoted philosopher Bertrand Russell: "The whole problem with the world is that fools and fanatics are always so sure of themselves and wiser people so full of doubt." In another column, "Wake up, America," I urged readers to educate themselves about how the Patriot Act was eroding our civil liberties and warned that the United States was becoming like the parent who says, "do as I say, not as I do" when it came to human rights and liberties.

I received a lot of angry mail, in which I was called, among other things, an "America-hating terrorist lover," a "communist" (even though I hadn't even touched on economic policy in the column), and my all-time favorite, someone who was "using the American Way of Life to destroy the American Way of Life and the Rest of Western Civilization in the process." (I was strangely proud of that last one. All that power from one 700-word column, when I couldn't even get my kids to put their clothes in the laundry basket! The pen really *is* mightier than the sword.)

There were common themes running through the angry letters I received: that I was unpatriotic—bordering on traitorous—for questioning government policy, and that anyone the government had deemed a terrorist suspect had no right to due process and deserved whatever treatment they got.

Let's take a look at what I believe is a pivotal passage in *Mockingjay*, the one where we not only see some of the same ethical dilemmas being raised, but also where it became clear to me that Katniss could never end up with Gale. Katniss visits Beetee and Gale in the Special Defense area, where they are working on designs for new weapons, and recognizes Gale's twitch-up snare from their times hunting for sustenance in the woods of District 12. Beetee and Gale are adapting the ideas behind Gale's traps into weapons for use against humans. What disturbs Katniss most is the psychology behind the weapons—that they are talking about placing booby-trapped explosives near food and water supplies and, even worse, creating two-stage devices that result in greater destruction of life by playing on that most human of emotions: compassion. The first bomb goes off, and then when rescue workers come in to aid the wounded and dying, a secondary device explodes.

Katniss gives voice to her unease about this strategy:

"That seems to be crossing some kind of line," I say. "So anything goes?" They both stare at me—Beetee with doubt,

Gale with hostility. "I guess there isn't a rule book for what might be unacceptable to do to another human being."

"Sure there is. Beetee and I have been following the same rule book President Snow used when he hijacked Peeta," says Gale.

Gale's "they do it, so why shouldn't we?" response reminded me of mail I got after a column I wrote following revelations of abuses by the U.S. military at Abu Ghraib prison. Several writers questioned why I was so concerned about those imprisoned at Abu Ghraib after what "they" did to us on 9/11. Never mind that in all likelihood the inhabitants of Abu Ghraib had nothing whatsoever to do with 9/11, or that, according to an International Committee of the Red Cross report dated February 2004, military intelligence officers estimated that "between 70 to 90 percent of persons deprived of their liberty in Iraq had been arrested by mistake."

One writer asked me how I, as a Jew, could feel badly about what happened at Abu Ghraib, when Nicholas Berg, a Jewish contractor working in Iraq, had recently been beheaded. I found the question astonishing, because to me, it was a non sequitur. The murder of Nick Berg was horrifying in the extreme. I would have found it equally abhorrent had he been a Christian or a Muslim, a Sikh or a Hindu or an atheist. Like Katniss, I feel that there are certain absolutes, lines that cannot be crossed without giving up one's own humanity. Although I hadn't agreed with the invasion of Iraq in the first place, I'd wanted to believe President Bush when he said: "Iraq is free of rape rooms and torture chambers." I honestly didn't believe that when he said that, what he *really* meant was, "Iraq is free of *Saddam Hussein's* torture chambers—ours, on the other hand, are now open." To me, the murder of Nick Berg in no way excused the behavior of the

U.S. soldiers at Abu Ghraib, or the culture from the top of the Bush administration down, that enabled it. Torturing prisoners in response to a horrifying act doesn't make us even. It just means that more horrifying acts have occurred.

As Katniss observes, there is no "rule book," but across all faiths and creeds there is some version of "The Golden Rule"— "Do unto others as you would have done unto yourself."

This principal of faith has also been codified into civil law. Our Founding Fathers wrote a prohibition against "cruel and unusual punishment" into the Eighth Amendment of the Constitution. In modern times, in response to some of the worst atrocities in the first half of the twentieth century, the United Nations created a series of international laws and treaties in an attempt to prevent any recurrence. One of these is Common Article 3 of the 1949 Geneva Convention, which prohibits "violence to life and person," in particular "mutilation, cruel treatment and torture," and also prohibits "outrages upon personal dignity, in particular humiliating and degrading treatment."

In 1984, the UN General Assembly adopted the Convention Against Torture, which the United States signed in April 1988 and ratified in October 1994. This treaty prohibits extraditing or deporting any person to a country where they will face a significant risk of torture. Yet under the Bush administration, our government engaged in the practice of *extraordinary rendition*, sending detainees on secret flights to Egypt, Morocco, Syria, and Jordan, all of which have been known to condone torture within their borders and have been cited by our own State Department for human rights violations.

Many of my columns touched on such policies, questioning if they really contributed to our security (because real life is not like the TV series *24*, and moral issues aside, there is no scientific evidence to prove that torture is an effective method of obtaining actionable intelligence) and further, if such policies were consistent with our values as Americans. No matter how we choose to phrase it, our government didn't just break the Golden Rule; it broke U.S. and international law.

I believe that in order to support the use of torture one has to convince oneself, through hatred, that the person being tortured is subhuman, or else surrender a part of one's own humanity. Otherwise, it would not be possible to inflict that kind of pain and suffering on another. As I wrote in the Abu Ghraib column back in 2004:

> by framing this conflict as a struggle of good vs. "evil," [President Bush] rationalized the "anything goes in the War on Terror" philosophy, pushing this country down the slippery slope that led to the horrors of Abu Ghraib. . . once the principle that international law is for other people (but not us) is established, it's not such a big leap to the "serious violations of international humanitarian law. . . in some cases tantamount to torture" documented by the International Committee of the Red Cross (ICRC). History proved that when you start to consider others as untermenschen, humanity goes out the window.

Following this, one woman actually wrote to me asking me how I could say waterboarding was torture since it left no physical scars—there were "no broken bones" and it was "just water." And after all—these were *terrorists* we were talking about. The ends clearly justified the means for her, just as they do for Gale, Snow, and Coin.

Leaving aside the fact that waterboarding creates the sensation of drowning and therefore can hardly be considered "just water," Peeta's mental hijacking by the Capitol shows us that psychological torture can be equally as damaging as physical torture, and the effects harder to "cure." A 2007 ICRC study found that prisoners who had been tortured using techniques similar to waterboarding by the Chilean government under the dictatorship of General Pinochet still have persistent nightmares of drowning almost two decades later. Broken bones don't last nearly as long.

Like the readers of my columns, Gale can't understand why Katniss cares so much when she finds out that her prep team from the Capitol is being subjected to inhumane treatment by President Coin:

> The preps have been forced into cramped body positions for so long that even once the shackles are removed, they have trouble walking . . . Flavius' foot catches on a metal grate over a circular opening in the floor, and my stomach contracts when I think of why a room would need a drain. The stains of human misery that must have been hosed off these white tiles . . .

Even though they are residents of the Capitol, ostensibly her enemy, and even though she has survived both the Hunger Games and the Quarter Quell by killing others, Katniss cannot bear to think of Venia, Flavius, and Octavia being subjected to such treatment. Later, while out hunting, Gale asks her why she cares so much about the members of her prep team when they basically spent the last year "prettying [her] up for slaughter." Katniss struggles to explain, pointing out that none of them are evil or cruel, or even smart—she likens them to children.

Gale is completely unforgiving of their ignorance:

"They don't know what, Katniss?" he says. "That tributes
—who are the actual children involved here, not your trio of
freaks—are forced to fight to the death? That you were going
into that arena for people's amusement? Was that a big secret
in the Capitol?"

"No. But they don't view it the way we do," I say. "They're
raised on it and—"

"Are you actually defending them?". . .

"I guess I'm defending anyone who's treated like that for
taking a slice of bread. Maybe it reminds me too much of
what happened to you over a turkey!"

Still, he's right. It does seem strange, my level of concern
over the prep team. I should hate them and want to see them
strung up. *(Mockingjay)*

Katniss "should" hate them. But why? Is that not one of the
cruelest fallacies of war? That everyone, just by the virtue of
being "other," is different and irredeemably bad? Katniss *should*
have the most reasons to hate, having been sent into the arena
not once, but twice. But despite everything she's been through,
she's still capable of seeing the so-called "enemy" as individuals,
rather than as a monolithic entity. She remembers that Octavia
snuck her a roll rather than see her hungry and that Flavius had
to quit during the Quarter Quell because he couldn't stop
crying.

Gale, on the other hand, is incapable of doing this. And in
our own society, this inability to individuate within a religious
or racial group is how we end up with the bizarre and painful
irony of watching even Juan Williams, the same African-
American journalist who wrote: "Racism is a lazy man's sub-
stitute for using good judgment," declaring on Fox News:

"When I get on the plane, I got to tell you, if I see people who are in Muslim garb and I think, you know, they are identifying themselves first and foremost as Muslims, I get worried. I get nervous."

Throughout the Hunger Games series, Katniss' feelings swing between Gale and Peeta, and the differences between the two are crystallized in this final book by the polar opposite ways they deal with their grief over the destruction of District 12 and everything that has happened leading up to this point. Gale wants revenge at any cost, by any means necessary—and, if you believe the rebellion responsible for the bombs that explode outside Snow's mansion, ultimately that cost is very dear, resulting in the death of Katniss' beloved sister, Prim, along with many other people's sisters and brothers. Thus the series comes full circle: the reason Katniss volunteered to be a tribute in the first volume was in order to save her sister's life—an act of courage that ultimately proves in vain. The Capitol did horrible things to many, many people—but by choosing to play by the same horrific rules, the rebellion actually causes the same kind of tragedy it was intended to prevent.

I've been very angered by reviews in which Peeta is called a "wimp," because I actually think he's the braver of the two boys. Why? Because Peeta is the one who, despite everything he's been through—the Hunger Games, the Quarter Quell, physical and psychological torture—is able to retain his essential humanity. Peeta is the one who, unlike Gale, recognizes there is a line that must never, *ever* be crossed. That is why he's the one that Katniss must end up with in order to stay true to herself and be able to heal and find some measure of happiness—happiness that Gale, with his moral ambivalence and quest for vengeance, could never have provided.

Some of the people I admire most in the world are Marianne Pearl, the wife of murdered journalist Daniel Pearl (who was beheaded in 2002 by Pakistani kidnappers while researching a story), and Judea Pearl, Danny's father. Ms. Pearl, whom I was fortunate enough to meet last year, and her in-laws are people who could so easily have gone down the same path Gale did, and it would have been hard to blame them. But instead they have honored Daniel's life work by continuing to work toward cross-cultural understanding through the creation of the Daniel Pearl Foundation.

The results of a path of revenge, as Katniss observes to the mineworker in *Mockingjay*, is that "it just goes around and around, and who wins? Not us. Not the districts. Always the Capitol."

Not just the Capitol. We're meant to think that Snow and Coin are opposites, but as we learn by the end of *Mockingjay*, Coin's name is no accident. The leaders are, as the old saying goes, two sides of the same coin.

In the summer of 2008, two letters from readers arrived at my paper. One, addressed to me, asked, "Can you name me an instance where you are on the United States' side on an issue?" The other, addressed to my editor at the paper, complained: "If you're going to continue to publish the far left ramblings of Sarah Darer Littman on your editorial page, you can at least try to balance things out by having somebody else on who actually wants to see our country win the war on terrorism."

I found myself bemused by both, because as far as I'm concerned, I'm on the United States' side on EVERY issue. It's because I love my country so much, because I believe so passionately in the ideals upon which it was founded, that I'm so vocal when I feel that our government and our elected officials are taking us down paths that diverge from those principles.

So what does it mean to be patriotic? What does "being on America's side" constitute? Does it make "my country"—or in

Katniss' case, the rebellion—"right or wrong"? Personally, I don't believe that is the case. One of the greatest minds of all time, Albert Einstein, said, "Unthinking respect for authority is the greatest enemy of truth."

To me, it is about asking questions, fighting for what you believe in, and holding our leaders accountable. It's about making sure that they don't take us down a path that is antithetical to what we stand for. It's about saying, "The United States does not torture. It's against our laws, and it's against our values," as President Bush declared in a speech on September 6, 2006, but really *meaning* it, not coming up with rationalizations for how and why we are allowed do so.

It's about facing the real challenges ahead of us without losing who we are as a nation, without compromising the core values and beliefs that made America the shining beacon of democracy in the world.

I have a letter to the editor from a World War II veteran, Richard P. Petrizzi, that I keep pinned above my desk. It reads: "I have many friends who are veterans who have never worn a flag on their lapels or flown flags in front of their homes. Yet these same people went to war to fight the dictators who were trying to conquer the world. We fought at that time to preserve our freedoms, including freedom of speech. I urge Sarah Darer Littman to keep writing her column and standing up for what democracy is all about."

Almost two thousand years ago, the poet Juvenal wrote the Satires, a series of poems highly critical of the mores and actions of his Roman contemporaries. In "Satire X," he writes of the downfall of the head of the Praetorian Guard, Sejanus, and the reaction of the citizens of Rome as he is dragged through the streets to his execution. One citizen asks, "But on what charge was he condemned? Who informed against him?

What was the evidence, who the witnesses, who made good the case?"

Another replies: "Nothing of the sort; a great and wordy letter came from Capri;" in other words, Sejanus had been condemned to death on the basis of a letter from the Emperor Tiberius, because he'd fallen out of favor with his former friend. "Good; I ask no more," replies the first citizen—abandoning law and order to the winds.

Juvenal rails that "the people that once bestowed commands, consulships, legions and all else, now meddles no more and longs eagerly for just two things—Bread and Games!"

Or, in the original Latin: *Panem et Circenses*. The phrase originated with Juvenal, and two thousand years later, it describes how much of the American public preferred to lose themselves in "reality TV" than pay attention the erosion of civil liberties during the War on Terror; "asking no more" in the way of evidence from their government when confronted by policies that so clearly contradict our laws and our national values. From warrantless wiretapping of American citizens to the politicized hiring and firing of Department of Justice officials, from the abrogation of international treaties such as the Geneva Conventions and the UN Convention Against Torture to leaking the name of a covert CIA agent for political purposes—the list of Bush administration transgressions goes on. Although the Obama administration has corrected some of the worst abuses, such as the use of torture, it still hasn't rejected the use of extraordinary rendition or closed the prison at Guantanamo Bay, despite the fact that the harsh treatment received there has motivated several released prisoners to become members of Al-Qaeda in the Arabian Peninsula. Yet much of the American public remains too busy watching TV, preferring to discuss *Dancing with the Stars* and *Jersey Shore*, and continues to accept the harsh treatment of prisoners under the guise of "national security" without understanding the global strategic implications, let alone the moral ones.

Plutarch compares the Capitol to ancient Rome (and thus the United States) in *Mockingjay*: "In the Capitol, all they've known is Panem et Circenses. . . . The writer was saying that in return for full bellies and entertainment, his people had given up their political responsibilities and therefore their power."

In Collins' series, despite her youth and attempts by both sides to manipulate her for their own ends, Katniss refuses to give up her power. Her suicide threat in *The Hunger Games* gives direct challenge to President Snow on nationwide television, forcing him to declare Peeta and Katniss co-winners of the Seventy-fourth Games. In *Catching Fire*, Katniss helps harness the lightning meant to torment the tributes in the Quarter Quell and uses it to destroy the Arena's force field. Finally, in *Mockingjay*, after Coin proposes a new Hunger Games and Katniss realizes that the end result of the rebellion has been merely to replace one amoral leader with another, she aims her arrow upward and shoots Coin dead. (Granted, it's a sad reflection of the violence that she's experienced in her short life and her complete distrust of the entire political structure of Panem—one that threw her into the Hunger Games arena in the first place—that she feels assassination is the only answer. We are fortunate, in contrast, to live in a country where we are free to express our unhappiness with the status quo through less drastic means.)

The BookPage blog asked Suzanne Collins: What do you hope these books will encourage in readers? Her answer: "I hope they encourage debate and questions. Katniss is in a position where she has to question everything she sees. And like Katniss herself, young readers are coming of age politically." In an interview on the Scholastic website, Collins said she hoped that readers would come away with "questions about how elements of the book might be relevant in their own lives. And, if they're disturbing, what they might do about them."

I consider *Mockingjay* a brilliant book for our time. Not only does it raise the difficult, eternal questions of war and humanity, grief and revenge, but one hopes it will encourage all of us to become more politically aware and active, and not to ever allow ourselves to risk the erosion of our democracy and civil liberties for *panem et circenses*.

SARAH DARER LITTMAN *is an award-winning author of middle-grade and young adult novels, including* Confessions of a Closet Catholic, Purge, Life, After, *and the upcoming* Want to go Private? *In addition to writing for teens, she is a columnist for Hearst Newspapers (CT) and writes for the political websites CTNewsJunkie.com and MyLeftNutmeg.com.*

The goal of every culture is to decay through over-civilization; the factors of decadence—luxury, skepticism, weariness and superstition—are constant. The civilization of one epoch becomes the manure of the next.

—Cyril Connolly

The Hunger Games trilogy deals with many themes: war, rebellion, the manipulation of media. But it was its concern with societal decadence and its inevitable downfall that made the first book's release timely. The bestselling YA dystopian series came onto shelves just as the world's economy took a tumble. For years we'd been living in comfort and excess. Consumerism was rife, and shows like *Sex and the City* glorified consumption by extolling the virtues of shoes worth hundreds of dollars. Then, suddenly, the party was over, and the world became concerned with trying to save money rather than spend it. Today the idea of wasteful consumption turns our stomachs.

It isn't as if this is the first time our society has gone from a period of great decadence to a time of recession; the pattern seems to be predictable. Yet despite the fact that rampant self-indulgence never lasts, those in the moment still somehow manage to think it can. Why is it that those in power truly believe that this time, this time, decadence will win out? Probably because decadence can be so much darn fun. The problem is, in order for these few people to continue to live this kind of lifestyle, many others must sacrifice a great deal of personal

THE INEVITABLE DECLINE OF DECADENCE

▶

ADRIENNE KRESS

Decadence is fun in theory: eating all of the ice cream yo[u]
whenever you want and having nothing to do but read an[d]
television and hang out with friends sounds great at first. B[ut]
you're busy indulging yourself, someone has to keep the world
smoothly. Someone has to do all that work you're avoiding, and c[hances]
are that they'd like the chance to indulge in a little decadence
Adrienne Kress explains, Panem is a perfect example of a soci[ety]
lives to excess, as well as the perfect example of excess' in[evitable]
result.

freedom. And it is the dissatisfaction of the many forced to make this sacrifice that inevitably leads to the decadent society's downfall.

First, before we look at the books themselves, a definition of decadence is in order. Most of us think of decadence as being a matter of pure indulgence. Going to the spa. Sleeping in past noon. Being fed chocolates by a handsome young man while another fans you with a large palm leaf. That kind of thing—a moment of pure selfishness, where a person's own desires are met. And truly, there isn't anything wrong with going to the spa, or sleeping in, or being fed chocolates—once in a while. It can be a huge release to take a moment to do something that has no practical purpose aside from relaxing the body and indulging the senses.

Decadence in and of itself is not necessarily a bad thing. In fact it's probably even a necessary thing, every so often, to experience a moment of indulgence, especially as so often we spend our lives working and doing things for others. A bit of selfishness can have remarkable restorative powers, allowing us to rejuvenate ourselves and carry on with the daily grind of life. It can be the reward for having to do something particularly trying. The dessert at the end of the healthy meal.

The trouble with decadence, like the trouble with most things, comes from over-indulging in it—a lack of moderation. To live a life that consists solely of decadent experiences would be to live a life that is very unproductive. Sleeping all day and then going to the spa and eating chocolates? When would you get anything practical done?

The other problem with decadence is that, after indulging, it can be difficult to go back to the regular grind of work. Why get up at seven-thirty in the morning to get chores done when you can sleep in? Why feed yourself when hunky guys can do it for you? (Okay, the whole hunky guy argument is rather solid. But I digress.) We have to live our lives. We have to make money so that we can put food on our table. We have to cultivate and grow that food in the first place.

What happens, then, when someone wants to live a decadent lifestyle all the time? Well, it means he has to find someone else to provide all the other stuff for him. He needs to find someone else to make the products that he is indulging in. He needs to find someone else to clean his apartment. To raise his children. Self-indulgence becomes the worst kind of team effort, the many working for the benefit of the one.

What's more, spending one's life focused solely on one's own pleasure, aside from affecting one's physical well being—sleeping all day, that can't be good for muscle strength—can also have an even more dangerous effect on the psyche. When a person's purpose in life becomes indulging himself, it's tempting to start believing that anything that gets in the way of the indulgence must be stopped, and anything that helps achieve it should be promoted. And when you care only about yourself, why should you care about the people who make it possible for you to indulge? Why should you care about your "team"?

This is how a world like the one in the Hunger Games series can come into being. But instead of being about an individual who is interested in self-indulgence, the books are about an entire society. Such a society isn't a fictional construct. We have seen such societies in the real world, as well. Ancient Rome was known for its decadent parties, where servants were on hand to wipe spittle from the faces of wealthy citizens indulging in feasts while reclining on couches in rooms with walls painted gold. The time of Marie Antoinette was well-known for extravagance, not only in clothes and food, but also in the complete indulgence of fantasy. The queen was infamous for so thoroughly not understanding the suffering and starvation of her people that, when told they had no bread to eat, she said, "Let them eat cake." She took this oblivious decadence to a whole new level when she had a miniature hamlet built at her palace of Versailles, adjacent to her villa Petit Trianon, where she could pretend to be a common shepherdess or milkmaid and enhance her fantasy by petting her animals, milking cows, even collecting eggs from chickens—playing at what was, for many of her subjects, a difficult daily reality.

What's worse, such societies can actually convince themselves that this self-indulgence of the few based on the work of the many can actually be a good thing for everyone. That it is better to curtail part of the population's rights and freedoms so that the society as a whole can remain intact.

In *The Hunger Games* the excuse is to prevent nuclear holocaust. We are told it almost happened once before, which is why District 13, the district that produced nuclear weaponry, was supposedly destroyed. The country now lives under the watchful eye and mighty thumb of the Capitol, not as a punishment, but to prevent total annihilation. A little suffering, the reasoning goes, is better than oblivion. It is better for all to work toward one positive goal, the supposed preservation of the country, and to give up certain personal freedoms such as how much one can eat or how laws are enacted and enforced, than to live a life that could destroy society. In the Hunger Games individual rights and freedoms are dangerous toys for a careless populace.

And, as any good child knows, if you can't play with your toys nicely, you lose them.

When we are first introduced to the dystopian future of the Hunger Games trilogy, the reader can easily draw the conclusion that we are being painted a picture of a gloomy impoverished future: a post-apocalyptic world where everyone must fend for themselves. Of course, we conclude this because we are introduced first to District 12, one of the poorest districts in the country. What we don't realize until later is that this series isn't about people surviving in a world where there are no commodities, but rather about a world where most exist in terrible conditions in order to support those who have great luxury and food aplenty. These lucky few simply don't live in the districts (though some districts do have more than others). These lucky few are the citizens in the Capitol, a city state reminiscent of ancient Rome.

Examples of decadence come to us in drips and drabs. The first indication that things are different elsewhere is Effie Trinket's colored wigs. The absurdity of her appearance is in stark contrast to that of the citizens of 12, who can barely afford to clothe themselves, let alone decorate themselves to no practical purpose. But our first example of true decadence is served on the train to the Capitol—in a very visceral moment when Katniss is presented with not only enough to eat, but too much.

Food is a huge metaphor in the books. The country is even called "Panem," which means "bread." Food is life. We learn that it is what initially brought Katniss and Peeta together as children when he saved her life by giving her slightly burnt bread. Food gave her hope when she and Gale were able to hunt and provide for her family. Food becomes a symbol of strength to her in the arena when, during her first Hunger Games, District 11 sends her bread as a gift of gratitude. Food is what keeps people alive. It's what shows others that they care. And so when we see food treated as trash, when we see people simply throw food away because they have too much of it, we understand that we are witnessing the ultimate display of decadence and overindulgence: life being tossed aside.

For each piece of food wasted, we the reader can only imagine how much that food would have helped someone in one of the districts. Nothing in the entire trilogy achieves a more disgusting display of decadence than the party in *Catching Fire*, where people eat as much as they possibly can only to vomit it back up so that they can eat more: "All I can think of is the emaciated bodies of the children on our kitchen table as my mother prescribes what the parents can't give . . . And here in the Capitol they're vomiting for the pleasure of filling their bellies again and again."

Here we have another clear allusion to ancient Rome, where it was commonplace to vomit up one's meal in order to partake of more—or at least to vomit post-meal after having partaken of too much. As Cicero is thought to have said of Julius Caesar: "[He] expressed a desire to vomit after dinner." As if eating until one threw up was the way things worked, and not representative of overindulgence.

Another demonstration of indulgence in the series is the luxury of taking care of one's outer self. For Katniss, clothes are a means to guard against the elements. Her one sentimental garment is her father's hunting jacket, and even it still serves a practical purpose. She does so little to take care of her appearance that her style team has to work very hard just to get her to a *starting point* of which they approve. We see in comparing her way of life to that of the Capitol how extreme its way of life really is. Not only do its citizens dress in extravagant clothes and wear ridiculous wigs, but they surgically alter their appearance by dyeing their skin bright colors and even by making themselves look like animals.

Of course, this obsession with superficiality should feel familiar to any of us reading these books. It reflects not only habits of the past, but our current modern obsessions. In ancient

Rome the citizens were wig-obsessed, as were those living in the Restoration Period in England and the time preceding the French Revolution, where women's wigs could reach upwards of three feet high. Even today, we see an obsession with hair pieces and extensions.

But the idea of surgically altering a person's appearance purely for aesthetic purposes is a truly modern idea. We cut and slice and dice ourselves and stitch it all back up together in an effort to look younger or more attractive. A sign of true wealth and decadence is a woman who is more plastic than flesh. And, of course, we have all seen the pictures of those who overindulged. Images of the "Cat Lady," a woman who attempted to look cat-like through surgery, became infamous around the world. It's hard not to think of her real life example when introduced to Tigris in the books, a character who exemplifies going too far—so far, in fact, that she is beyond ridicule, and instead we pity her.

As it stands in current society, the purpose of plastic surgery is to make a person appear as if she hasn't had any, unlike the characters in the Hunger Games about whose cosmetic surgery there can be no doubt. But is it that impossible to think things won't shift? After all, it used to be that we recognized older people because of the lines on their faces. Now we recognize the typical "rejuvenating" procedures: skin pulled back so tightly that there is little expression left on the face; work done around the eyes to make them look cavernous. Such an appearance used to be considered unnatural; people would gossip disdainfully about anyone who looked that way. But now the tell-tale tightness is becoming so common that people hardly notice it as unusual. What's to say adding a tail eventually wouldn't be considered just as normal? And fun to swoosh around.

Decadence is also seen in the neo-classical architecture of

Panem's grand columned buildings, reflecting the Roman influence once again. The purpose of the architecture in ancient Rome was to demonstrate Rome's power over the rest of the world, and its wealth. It was large, it was audacious, it was decadently decorated with frescos, friezes, and other forms of statuary, sometimes even painted in gold. We get glimpses of comparable architecture in *Catching Fire* at the celebration in the Capitol. The banquet room has forty-foot-high ceilings, musicians seemingly float on white clouds halfway up, the floor is covered with flower gardens and ponds are filled with exotic fish. And tables are replaced by sofas "so that people can eat and drink . . . in the utmost comfort" just as the ancient Romans did (*Catching Fire*).

And though not ancient Roman–inspired, architecture as decadence can also be seen in President Snow's greenhouse in *Mockingjay*. Such a building requires a great deal of upkeep and money to maintain, and the purpose of Snow's is not even food production—it's the ability to grow roses year round. Its description as too sweet, almost suffocating in its heat, is a great reminder of the excess it represents.

Thanks to the way the series begins, with Katniss in District 12, the reader has no doubt that behind all this decadence is a large population working to support it. Like the bottom row of cheerleaders in the pyramid, the job of the districts is to prop up the Capitol. Each district provides a particular resource to the rest of the country. Or so it is said. From the beginning of *The Hunger Games*, however, we know there is not enough food to go around, not enough building supplies to construct solid homes to protect people from the elements. Product is being made, but it is clear that the Capitol is getting the lion's share. None of it is being consumed by the districts.

We see even more grotesque examples of the many supporting the few, most notably with the Avoxes who serve at the pleasure of the Capitol's citizens. Yes, they are supposedly being punished for crimes by having their tongues cut out and being forced to work as slaves. But through Katniss we are well aware that the crimes they are being punished for are not always things such as murder and rape, but rather speaking out against the Capitol, or trying to run away from a horrible situation. Or being difficult. They are the perfect metaphor for the power structure of Panem: like the districts, they serve the Capitol in silent obedience.

Of course, you can't turn everyone into an Avox; You can't punish an entire population, though it appears the Capitol has tried to do just that. And when an entire population grows restless, the result is change. A society of workers who might be weak from lack of nutrition but still strong from day labor has a definite advantage over a society of overripe, unhealthy citizens who haven't lifted so much as a pen in recent memory.

What history has shown us is that a state of decadence simply can't last. Invariably such a society collapses. There are usually two ways the breakdown happens. The first takes place when the economy of the decadent society simply cannot support its citizens' lifestyle. When people spend more and indulge more than they actually can afford to do. We saw something similar happen recently, in the last recession. The drive to have "things" caused people to spend what they didn't have, and banks were granting loans to people who could not afford to pay them back. When a society is founded on a lie, like on fake money, well, that's not going to end too well. Like a house built on sand, eventually it's going to sink.

The other way that such a society comes tumbling down is through revolution. A system of the few living off the many simply cannot last. When the majority of people are the ones creating the products that sustain just a few people, in the end all those hard-working people are going to realize, "Hey, wait a minute. There are more of us than of them." History has witnessed this pattern time and time again. The fall of Rome. The French Revolution.

Usually it's a combination of both financial irresponsibility and the few holding down the many that leads to the inevitable fall.

So really it should come to no surprise to anyone in power that such a revolution takes shape in the world of the Hunger Games. After all, the Games themselves exist specifically to demonstrate the Capitol's power over the populace, to help prevent such a revolution from happening.

Thus the Games represent more than just the decadence of a society seeking greater and greater thrills. They are, at the same time, a demonstration of how to keep the masses in their place. But the Games also end up serving as a catalyst for revolution, a means to reach the millions of citizens whose shoulders are starting to ache horribly from holding up the rest of the pyramid.

Truly, it's been a long time since the title of a series was so apt. This really is the story of the Hunger Games.

Collins says it best in *Mockingjay* when she has Plutarch, in conversation with Katniss, directly reference Ancient Rome:

> "*Panem et Circenses* translates into 'Bread and Circuses'. The writer was saying that in return for full bellies and entertainment, his people had given up their political responsibilities and therefore their power."

> I think about the Capitol. The excess of food. And the ultimate entertainment. The Hunger Games.

The idea here is that, by entertaining the citizens of the Capitol, the government can distract them from realizing what it is doing to the rest of the country. Focusing on small details of the Games, on the odds of who will win, on the costumes worn by the contestants, and the excitement of the Games themselves replaces greater concerns over politics or the state of poverty elsewhere in the country—even the truly cruel nature of the Games themselves.

The Capitol isn't the only area being entertained to distraction, however. The goal is also to distract the districts. After all, you have to give people something to take their minds off their suffering or all they will do is dwell on it. And dwelling on it can lead to unpleasant results, like coming to the conclusion that it might be a neat idea to revolt.

So the Hunger Games become like the gladiator combats of old, set even in their own coliseum, though the arena for the Games is much more elaborate and the action is relayed not to an audience in the stands but rather to all of Panem with the help of television. Entertainment on a massive scale.

We can see how such distractions are used in our own society: the film boom in the '30s during the Great Depression, for example. And even now as our world is in serious financial trouble we have fantastical epic films rising in popularity. These films allow an audience to escape the less pleasant aspects of their lives compellingly and completely.

Not only does such entertainment distract during the actual Games, it also becomes something aspirational. So just as we have people today longing to be famous for no other reason than to be famous, the Hunger Games provide a similar opportunity. Not only is there pride and celebrity in being the winner of such a huge event broadcast to the entire population, there are the rewards given to the winning tribute's district as well, like extra food. So instead of the Games' being horrific events to try to avoid, for some—like the "Careers" in Districts 1 and 2, children who are trained from a young age to compete in the Games—it becomes a mark of honor to win. And yet ironically, by supporting the Games in order to earn such benefits as food rewards, these districts are supporting the very thing that keeps them down and prevents them from having enough food in the first place.

But of course, the Games' most nefarious purpose is to remind the masses who is in charge:

> As our yearly reminder that the Dark Days must never be repeated, [the government] gave us the Hunger Games . . . Whatever words they use, the real message is clear. "Look how we take your children and sacrifice them and there's nothing you can do. If you lift a finger we will destroy every last one of you." (*The Hunger Games*)

It is hard not to fear a power that can so easily, thoughtlessly sacrifice the lives of children. If they are willing to do that, well, what else might they do? Better to stay obedient and alive than risk a worse form of retaliation.

And yet, in the end, the Hunger Games become a message of good, the platform for revolution. Of course, Katniss doesn't realize how her small act of rebellion will start a greater one, but for people to see sacrifice in a place where everyone only indulges in their own selfish wants, her small gesture in threatening to eat the poisonous berries rather than killing Peeta to save herself is enough to spark hope in people. The metaphor of the girl catching fire is very apt.

However, the Hunger Games isn't telling the story of a society's return to goodness, of the fall from decadence to the rise of equality. It is instead telling our story—the story of our world and the continuous cycle civilization seems to spin over and over again. It isn't focused on black and white, good and bad, but rather on highlighting the grey. The saviors of the country—the rebels—are presented in stark contrast to the Capitol. On the one side we have President Snow, a man who epitomizes decadence turning to decay, who epitomizes wastefulness and indulgence. He's an overripe fruit verging on rotting, and even smells a little too sweet. Never has something as beautiful as a rose seemed so threatening and sickening.

On the other side we have Coin, the President of District 13 and the incarnation of pragmatism. Her world is one of strictly enforced limits, where everyone gets enough to eat, but only just enough. Pleasure is secondary to survival. In 13, citizens have their schedules dictated to them and must not indulge themselves in anything, an imposed restraint that is for the benefit of the community at large.

We see in Snow and Coin two ends of a spectrum who oddly have much in common. Both have a deep distrust of the masses and believe they must be kept on a tight leash. And when Coin, upon winning the war, suggests doing one last Hunger Games as a logical solution to show the citizens of the Capitol who's in charge now, well, we see the exact same rationale for the Games that Snow used.

Coin has so much in common with Snow that it is easy to envision a government with her in charge ending up in a familiar place. The people would be yet again subjected to harsh rules "for their own good," this time rules of self-restraint. They would eventually reach a breaking point and once more seek to change the way they are being forced to live. After so many years without any kind of luxury or indulgence, who wouldn't want to be a little selfish? A society of indulgence will slowly develop and the cycle of decadence and downfall will begin all over again.

The Hunger Games suggests the only way to break out of the cycle is a third choice: moderation. Neither Snow nor Coin. The world of *Mockingjay*'s epilogue is hardly one that is bright and new. But it is one where the Capitol no longer has power over the other districts, where District 12 shuts down the dangerous mines and turns to producing medicine instead, and where, importantly, the history of what happened before is taught. It is clear that this is a society that understands that remembering the mistakes of the past is the only way to prevent them from recurring in the future. But the biggest sign that the society has truly changed is the toppling of a symbol—the end of the Hunger Games.

Can a cycle ever truly be broken? Is society always doomed to repeat the patterns of the past? Certainly our own history seems to reflect that theory. Time and time again people indulge in decadence until we self-destruct, only to do it all over again. But the end of *Mockingjay* seems to suggest otherwise. Though many have found it bleak, I personally see a great deal of optimism. Suzanne Collins could have chosen to give us Coin as president, an example of a continuous pattern, mistakes just waiting to be made again. Instead she gives us a song. And children. And though "they play on a graveyard" (*Mockingjay*), the important thing is that they are free to play.

ADRIENNE KRESS *is a Toronto born actor and author. Her books are* Alex and the Ironic Gentleman *and* Timothy and the Dragon's Gate *(Weinstein Books). She is a theatre graduate of the University of Toronto and the London Academy of Music and Dramatic Arts in the*

UK. *Published around the world,* Alex and the Ironic Gentlemen *was featured in the* New York Post *as a "Post Potter Pick," as well as on the* CBS Early Show. *It won the Heart of Hawick Children's Book Award in the UK and was nominated for the Red Cedar. The sequel,* Timothy, *was nominated for the Audie and Manitoba Young Readers Choice Awards.*

Her debut YA novel, The Friday Society, *will be published by Dutton in 2012. Visit her website at www.adriennekress.com.*

COMMUNITY IN THE FACE OF TYRANNY

▶

How a Boy with a Loaf of Bread and a Girl with a Bow Toppled an Entire Nation

BREE DESPAIN

By the end of the first book, it's obvious to just about everybody that the Capitol made a mistake in letting Katniss take Prim's place in the Hunger Games. What isn't obvious is why. Katniss doesn't intentionally stir up dissent, and she certainly isn't the cause. The people of Panem were unhappy long before Katniss appeared on their television screens. So what is it about our heroine that makes her such a threat? Bree Despain suggests that the answer lies in Katniss' greatest skill—not her dexterity with a bow, but her knack for creating community wherever she goes.

Being a tyrant is easy, really. All you have to do is take away people's freedom. Many people in today's society take certain liberties for granted: freedom of speech, freedom to assemble, free commerce, free press, and more simple freedoms such as travel and easy communication—all things that make a community strong and viable. But what if in one swift movement all of these liberties were taken away? That's what the Capitol did to the districts of Panem. After the first unsuccessful rebellion of the districts against the Capitol seventy-five years ago, the Capitol retaliated by taking every measure it could to destroy the feeling of community within the districts and between the districts, controlling and isolating people in order to keep them from rebelling again.

The most literal meaning of community is "to give among each other." Essentially, to share something amongst a group—whether that's information (communication), goods, common goals, or a sense of family. If you destroy the ability, or simply the desire, to give or to share amongst a group of people, you will destroy the heart of the community. And if you destroy the heart of community and replace it with fear, then you will control the people.

The Capitol does this first by keeping many of the people in the districts on the brink of starvation. It controlled the food sources, outlawing hunting and forcing parents to sign over their children's potential futures (and any sense of security or innocence that should come from being a child) in exchange for tesserae food rations. Only a privileged few outside the Capitol, especially in the poorer districts, have enough money to buy goods from the baker and the butcher (and I imagine the candle-stick-maker). And those few aren't going to complain about the needs of the less fortunate for fear of losing their privileged status. The Capitol keeps the people hungry enough that all anyone has the energy to think about is how to feed themselves.

Second, the Capitol instituted public flogging and curfews, and trained dastardly "Peacekeepers" to watch the people's every move in order to force them to keep their heads down for fear of punishment. It surrounded the districts with giant electrified fences to keep people from interacting with, or traveling to, other districts. Almost all forms of long-distance communica-tion have ceased to exist throughout the districts, and what little is permitted (television propaganda, and the telephones in the victors' mansions) is constantly monitored. It is also apparent that within the Capitol itself, and parts of the districts, the people are monitored by cameras so they are not free to com-municate without reprisal.

The Capitol even instituted an "ultimate punishment" for major infractions: cutting out the offending person's tongue, therefore making him or her unable to communicate—and in result unable to function properly within the community. The Avox is removed from his/her family and forced into a life of slavery. The ultimate punishment is ultimate isolation.

Considering all this, the Capitol may seem like a shining city on a hill for budding despots everywhere. So where did it go wrong? What was the fatal mistake that lead to its down-fall?

There were two mistakes, actually: the institution of the Hunger Games, and allowing the existence of a teenage girl like Katniss Everdeen from a place like District 12.

The Hunger Games

When you first think about the concept of the Hunger Games, it may seem like the perfect way to instill ultimate fear in the hearts of district citizens. The Games were created to punish the districts for their original attempt at rebellion, and to remind them of the uselessness of trying to oppose the almighty Capitol. The districts must sacrifice their children, a most precious commodity in any community, to the Capitol's sick idea of amusement. The mostly defenseless children are then forced to isolate themselves and fight to the death in an arena for mandatory public viewing on television—therefore symbolizing to the districts' citizens the isolation and futility of their own lives.

The Capitol instituted the Hunger Games to create derision and strife among the districts by pitting them against each other and making them hope for the other districts' children to be slaughtered instead of their own. But as Laura Miller from the *New Yorker*'s review of the first two books in the Hunger Games trilogy points out, "the practice of carrying off a population's innocent children and commanding their parents to watch them be slaughtered for entertainment—wouldn't that do more to provoke a rebellion than to head one off?"

And that's exactly what happens—eventually. It is over seventy years in the making, not a huge amount of time considering how oppressed the people of the districts are, but eventually (or inevitably) the Hunger Games play a major role in the demise of the Capitol. If it weren't for the Hunger Games and the resulting "victory tour" of the winner each year, the citizens of the individual districts would know nothing about the other districts except for the propaganda they are taught in school.

The rest of the year, it's almost as if the other districts don't even exist, but during the Games, each district is given a human face (or two human faces). Often those faces are not friendly ones, considering that the tributes are fighting to the death. That the only time the districts' inhabitants interact is when they're trying to kill each other plays right into the Capitol's calculating design. But the other tributes are human faces none-theless—ones that could possibly remind the people that they are not alone—and that's a big risk. Each district is given champions to rally behind—but if there was someone, or even a team of champions, who multiple districts could actually get behind, it would give the people a common bond, a sense of "community" to bring them together. And when that champion turns out to be someone who dares defy the Capitol—well, that's all it takes to spark a rebellion.

Katniss Everdeen: The Girl Who Should Never Have Existed . . .

The Capitol probably never thought a teenage girl like Katniss Everdeen could start an uprising with a fistful of berries—and she had no idea, either. But Katniss isn't really responsible for what happens that last day in the Games. The Capitol is. After all, it created Katniss in first place.

Collins tells us in an interview with Rick Margolis in *School Library Journal*:

Katniss is . . . a girl who should never have existed . . . the Capitol just thinking that [District] 12 is not ever really going to be a threat because it's small and poor, they create an environment in which Katniss develops, in which she is created, this girl who slips under this fence, which isn't electrified, and learns to be a hunter. Not only that, she's a survivalist, and along with that goes a degree of independent thinking that is unusual in the districts.

So here we have her arriving in the arena in the first book, not only equipped as someone who can keep herself alive in this environment—and then once she gets the bow and arrows, can be lethal—but she's also somebody who already thinks outside the box . . . And this new creature evolved, which is the mockingjay, which is Katniss.

One of President Snow's greatest mistakes, the one that led to the downfall of the Capitol, was his lack of attention to District 12. It seems as though the Capitol started out equally stringent in each of the districts (Katniss' mother occasionally refers to much darker days in the past) but over time it became lax in 12. After all, 12 is the poorest, hungriest district, without even much hope of winning the Hunger Games to bring in more food rations. The poorer citizens in that district are relegated to the Seam, where they have almost nothing to look forward to other than living and dying in the mines. And as the most downtrodden of the districts, 12 was pretty much ignored by the Capitol. It wasn't worth wasting precious resources on, such as electricity, so the fence was rarely a threat to anyone who dared go under it. It wasn't worth wasting the best Peacekeepers on either, so after a while, the Capitol stopped caring to send disciplined and obedient Peacekeepers there. This fostered an environment where a black market could exist, providing a gathering place for the people to exchange goods and information. A place where a budding sense of community was allowed to grow—even between the braver townsfolk who visited the market and the Peacekeepers who came for food and enjoyment.

At the beginning of *The Hunger Games*, most people in 12 are still too afraid to take advantage of the lapses of the Capitol's judgment concerning their district, but out of this negligent environment comes an unlikely heroine named Katniss Everdeen: a girl with an uncanny (and often unwitting) ability to create a sense of community wherever she goes.

Originally, when looking back at the text of the first Hunger Games book, I was tempted to say that the first act of community in the novel (after Katniss' father died) that helped Katniss become the kind of person she was before she was even reaped for the Hunger Games, was when she formed a hunting alliance with Gale. Instead of fending for themselves, they worked together to share the burden of feeding their loved ones. The "glue of mutual need" bonded them together, and they created not only a community—giving among each other—but the strongest form of community that exists: a family. But what dawned on me after rereading all three books in the trilogy again, was that the first "act of community in the face of tyranny" that was the catalyst for who Katniss became as a person was an act of community she was the *recipient* of—rather than the creator of. It was the incident involving "the boy with the bread."

After Katniss' father died in a mining accident and her mother went crazy with grief, Katniss and her sister, Prim, began to starve to death. Without their father to hunt, trade at the Hob, or provide income for the family, it looked like all was lost. In the downtrodden Seam, there was no one who had food to spare, and no one Katniss knew of who would have been willing to spare it if they had it. As Katniss tells us, because of the oppression of the Capitol, children die of starvation daily in the Seam. But just when Katniss was about to give up, to sit down and die like the Capitol would have wanted her to, Peeta Mellark, the baker's son, saw her need and decided to give what he could. He risked a beating from his tyrant of a mother by burning a few precious loaves of bread and then gave them to Katniss instead of throwing them out like he was instructed. This small act of kindness, of true community, was what helped bring Katniss back from the dead—and back to her senses.

With her hunger lessened for a moment, she was able to realize that she could buck the system, too—defy the Capitol—and slip under the non-electrified fence in order to hunt for her family. There she used the descriptions in the book her father created documenting plants that were safe to eat—his attempt at communicating his knowledge to his family before he was gone—to find food and medicine. There she formed the hunting alliance with Gale that kept both of their families alive and healthy, found enough hope to help her mother slowly recover from her depression, and learned to survive—and to kill. She became somewhat of a small hero to her district even before she was a tribute for the Hunger Games. She provided meat for the privileged in 12, as well as for the starving. She procured herbs to heal the sick, and she befriended the Peacekeepers as well as the ruffians. Around her, small shoots of community began to thrive.

And that was the Capitol's fatal mistake. Allowing Katniss to become, well, Katniss. Where was the hand of tyranny to crush this early uprising that consisted of a teen girl and her bow? Where was the electricity to keep her out of the woods? Where were the brutal Peacekeepers who should have beaten the spirit out her?

Yes, the Capitol, through its lapses in District 12, created Katniss Everdeen. The girl who cares enough to volunteer for the Hunger Games to save her sister. The girl who promises to try to win so she can return to her family and bring food to her district. The girl who unwittingly captures the love of her prep team and stylists, who then turn her into the "girl who was on fire." The girl who *befriends* Rue (rather than just making an alliance out of convenience like others in the Games before them), an opponent from a rival district who another tribute might have killed without regard. The girl who proves that friendship by caring for Rue as a sister and placing flowers on her body when she dies in order to rebuke the Capitol's Game-makers—an act that inspires District 11 to do something that has never been done before: send a gift to a tribute who isn't from their district. The girl who shows a nation that its members can work together rather than feel isolated from each other. The girl whose partnership and "romance" with Peeta gives the districts champions to really root for and feel connected to. The girl who creates a community bond within and between the districts. The girl whose defiance at the end of book one makes her and Peeta the symbol of a partnership—one so strong that President Snow will stop at nothing, including altering Peeta's memories, to try to destroy it—that can be formed to defy the Capitol. The Capitol created the girl who becomes the Mockingjay.

The girl who incites a rebellion that topples the government.

Too Little, Too Late

The problem with allowing a sense of community to spring up in an otherwise oppressed society is that once it has started to take root, it's almost impossible to stamp out. When President Snow sees what one girl and a trick with a handful of berries can do (make the Capitol look foolish and weak and incite uprisings among the people) he scrambles to stop the effects. He goes straight for the heart of Katniss' community, starting with invading the privacy of her home. He threatens her family if she doesn't try to help undo the damage that she has caused, then sends in terrible Peacekeepers to torment the citizens in order to force them back in line. The Hob, the community center, is burned to the ground, the fence is re-electrified, and the promised prize rations of food for District 12 are purposely spoiled. Seeing the suffering of her community, Katniss tries to do what President Snow asks. She tries to calm the rebellion, but as President Snow informs her, her efforts are too little, too late. Rebellion is spreading.

But really, it is President Snow who is doing too little, too late. At this point, it seems like anything he tries to do to squelch the feeling of community only fuels it in most of the districts. He even goes as far as to force Katniss to model her wedding dresses for the nation, only to announce that same day the show airs that Katniss, Peeta, and past victors are to be forced back into the arena. This should have broken their spirits, shown that not even the victors are safe or powerful, but it only serves to enrage the people more. And it gives secret rebels, such as Plutarch Heavensbee, the opportunity to manipulate the Games in order to further the cause of the rebellion. Although her involvement in Plutarch's plan is unwitting at first, it is still Katniss' uncanny ability to not only create a community, but a family, around her that fuels the ongoing uprisings. Katniss again blurs the lines between alliance and friendship by choosing to ally herself with people who seem supposedly weak (such as Beetee, Wiress, and Mags) because she cares about them, and many of the other contestants rally around Katniss because they know that she's the Mockingjay—the symbol of the power of the people to bond together and take down the Capitol. These unlikely friends are slowly welcomed into Katniss' ever-expanding family.

When Katniss breaks free of the arena, President Snow tries to retaliate with what feels like the ultimate blow—he attempts to destroy Katniss' community altogether by firebombing District 12. But even this horrible move seems to be too little, too late as Katniss' family escapes the bombings and is rescued by the mysterious inhabitants of District 13.

President Coin, A Different Kind of Tyrant

Even though my heart ached for Peeta, knowing he was a prisoner of Snow, I have to admit that during the months between finishing *Catching Fire* and the release of *Mockingjay* I felt somewhat reassured that everything was going to turn out fine once Katniss and her rag-tag family of Gale, Haymitch, her mother, Prim, Finnick, and the other surviving tributes made it to District 13. In fact, in my outline for this essay (which was written a couple of months before *Mockingjay* was released) I actually wrote the description for this portion of the essay to "discuss what happens in book three as far as community is concerned (the community that has bonded together in District 13) and how they take down the Capitol."

Part of me fully expected that Katniss would willingly take on her position as the Mockingjay, and with the help of the good-natured community in District 13, they'd take on the Capitol, free Peeta in the process, and take down President Snow. Then Katniss, their beloved general, would be asked (much like George Washington) to become the new leader of the united districts! The task would be difficult, but because of her ability to create community around her Katniss would be the perfect woman for the job—and the wonderful leaders of District 13 would help her do it.

Only once I opened the pages of *Mockingjay*, I discovered, along with Katniss, just how complicated the community in District 13 could be. What appears at first glance to be somewhat of a Utopian community that rose out of the ashes of the Capitol's attack—running with precision and efficiency to meet the needs of its people—suddenly seems a bit off when you look at it more closely.

Maybe it is the way they stamp the characters' not-to-be-deviated-from schedules on their arms, how everyone is called "soldier," that their jobs are selected for them by the government, the stringent way they control food portions, the fact that no one is allowed onto the surface without permission, how their locations are constantly monitored, or how no one gathers for an event unless told to do so by the president. It can be claimed that all of this is done for everyone's safety, to keep the community alive—and rightfully so—but at the same time, this just seems to be another way to rule by fear. By manipulation.

It slowly becomes very clear that President Coin is a tyrant in her own right—not as openly as President Snow, but perhaps even more insidiously. The first real clue of Coin's true nature is the fact that Katniss' prep team (part of her strange hodgepodge of a family) are treated like dangerous criminals—even animals—after they are kidnapped by the leaders of 13 to help with the Mockingjay propos. But I knew for sure that Coin was not to be trusted when Katniss has to fear that Peeta might be executed for his anti-rebellion speeches even though it is clear that he is being forced to participate against his will. This seemed like another one of Coin's manipulations—treat everyone like a threat to the citizens of 13, even their hero from the Hunger Games—and a great way to force Katniss to follow Coin's plans in exchange for Peeta's immunity.

Katniss poses a threat to both tyrannical leaders in Panem. However, while Snow attacks Katniss openly through trying to break her bond with Peeta—hijacking Peeta's brain and attempting to destroy his love for her—Coin attacks Katniss through manipulating her bonds with her family (forcing her obedience in exchange for the immunity of her victor friends), and then attempting to dispose of her when she poses less of a threat as a dead martyr than as a living symbol.

But it isn't until Katniss suspects that President Snow may be telling the truth about Coin's alleged final manipulation— that she was the one who ordered the blowing up of the Capitol children and then the rebel medics (including Prim) who tried to help them, and then tried to pass it off as the Capitol who committed the offense—that the real worst tyrant may have been revealed. President Snow preys on the sensibilities of community with the idea that a barricade of children around his mansion would slow the onslaught of the rebel forces, since it would take someone truly depraved to kill children in order to get to him. It's something the Mockingjay wouldn't do— but Coin apparently would. Although it's never confirmed that Coin is truly behind the bombing of the children, I believe this action is not only Coin's final blow against the Capitol, but also the ultimate manipulation of her own people, and that sacrificing Prim in the middle of it—destroying one of Katniss's deepest community connections—is meant to break Katniss.

And it almost does.

Rebuilding

Honestly, I was angry at first by how broken Katniss was after the climax of the trilogy. I cheered when Katniss shot Coin through the heart for her alleged evil deed. But then I still expected Katniss to become the George Washington of Panem. I wanted her to vanquish the foe and then become the new leader of a new nation. But in the end, she is so broken it's shocking . . . although not surprising considering that most dystopian stories end with a dead or destroyed protagonist. Collins even tells us in that interview from *School Library Journal* that the story is based in part on the tragic tale of Spartacus:

> . . . the historical figure of Spartacus really becomes more
> of a model for the arc of the three books, for Katniss . . .
> [Spartacus] was a gladiator who broke out of the arena and led
> a rebellion against an oppressive government . . . He caused
> the Romans quite a bit of trouble. And, ultimately, he died.[1]

Instead of killing Katniss, Collins, possibly following the lead of another ancient Roman war hero named Cincinnatus "who was called from his plow to rescue the republic and then returned to his fields after the danger had passed,"[2] chooses to send Katniss back to the desolation of the demolished District 12. Katniss is left there alone, with only a drunken Haymitch for company, in a place where there seems to be nothing left for

---

1. Supposedly, Spartacus was killed in the final battle of the war when he and his rebels attacked the Roman army, although his body was never found. The surviving rebels were crucified by Roman soldiers.

2. And who was a great inspiration to George Washington. Quote from William Calhoun, "Washington at Newburgh," *The Claremont Institute*.

her. No more ragtag family to rally around. Katniss has literally lost Prim, Finnick is dead, along with most of the members of the star squad, her mother and Gale have gone off to help with the transition of Panem, and Peeta's once unwavering love seems to have been irreparably damaged by President Snow's brainwashing.

While I was surprised by this turn of events, it feels fitting that the girl who should have never existed was sent back to the place that created her—a place that no longer exists, itself. It's even more fitting that Peeta—the boy with the bread, the person who made the first connection to her all those years before when she was almost destroyed by the tyranny of the Capitol the first time—is the person who eventually returns to 12 to help her recover. Together, as part of her therapy, they work on her father's book, expanding it with their own knowledge—communicating what they've learned in all the horror that could possibly save future generations from suffering as they did. As their bonds strengthen, they eventually create a new family. One strong enough to help rebuild the community of District 12 that once seemed lost forever. And if they can help it, one that will never be lost again.

The Hunger Games trilogy—what starts out as a tome depicting an example of ultimate totalitarian control—soon unravels into a possible morality tale for anyone with tyrannical aspirations, in which the concept of community is offered as the answer to overthrowing an oppressive regime. President Snow learns the hard way that any sense of true community must be stamped out in order for the dominant regime to remain in control. Overlooking the smallest act of community can light the spark that sets an entire neighborhood, or even nation, ablaze with feelings of brotherhood, sharing, and concern for the greater good. Even the weak, the broken, and the seemingly incapable pose a serious risk to a leader who rules out of fear. And although President Coin understands the power of community, and learns to manipulate it to get what she wants, even she learns that she can only push it so far before it snaps back and destroys her as well. They are both undone by a boy with a loaf of bread and a girl with bow.

BREE DESPAIN *is the author of* The Dark Divine, The Lost Saint, *and an upcoming third novel in the Dark Divine trilogy. Bree rediscovered her childhood love for creating stories when she took a semester off college to write and direct plays for at-risk inner-city teens from Philadelphia and New York. She currently lives in Salt Lake City, Utah, with her husband, two young sons, and her beloved TiVo.*

ACKNOWLEDGMENTS

Many thanks to Dee Liou, Jody He, and Amy Murphy from Hunger Games Trilogy: Unofficial Fansite (www.hunger gamestrilogy.com) for their assistance with the manuscript!